Stories of the Nations

Volume 2: From Count Bismarck to Queen Elizabeth II

by Lorene Lambert

With additional material from *The Child's Story of the Nations* by Charles Morris, originally published in 1901

Stories of the Nations, Volume 2: From Count Bismarck to Queen Elizabeth II

ISBN 978-1-61634-171-8 print
ISBN 978-1-61634-172-5 electronic download

Published and printed by
Simply Charlotte Mason, LLC
P. O. Box 892
Grayson, Georgia 30017-0892

Cover design: John Shafer

SimplyCharlotteMason.com

Contents

A Few Words with My Young Friends

No one can know what history means, or what the progress of the world has been, unless he knows a great deal about the recent centuries. We call them Early Modern and Modern Times. They have been centuries of invention. Years ago men did the most of their work with their hands; now they do the most of it with machines. They have been centuries of science. Years ago men knew very little about the great forces and forms of the universe; now they know a great deal about electricity and light and heat and a hundred other things. They have been centuries of progress in human liberty. The slaves of hundreds of years ago are free today, and the people of the nations have far more liberty than they had in the past ages.

The recent centuries have been crowded with marvels, full of great events and wonderful discoveries. They have had their triumphs of war and their greater triumphs of peace; their great warriors and their greater statesmen; their great doers and their greater thinkers. Man's hands have been busy, but his brain has been busier, and the triumphs of the recent centuries are the triumphs of the mind.

I hope the readers of this little book understand what I have just said. If any part of it is not clear to them they must read on to the end to learn what it all means.

The stories of the nations are stories of people who were living on the Earth during the days of our grandfathers, and their fathers, and their fathers' fathers before them. Some of the stories are long and some are short, but all of them are stories of real people—their lives and their acts and how they affected all those around them. Of course I cannot tell about every person who lived on the earth, but I hope this little history—and the one that comes before it by the same name—will help you feel that you know some of them.

That is all I have to say here. One cannot say everything in an introduction. And none of you, when you are invited to a good dinner, care much to be told what is on the table. You would rather find out for yourselves. So with these few words I throw open the doors of the dining hall, and let you in to the feast of good things which has been prepared for you.

Chapter 1

The Modern World

I f I were to say to you, "We live in the modern world," would you agree with me? After all, fast automobiles crowd our streets; jet airplanes soar through our skies; satellites circle our globe, beaming their signals here and there; and clever computers help everything in our world to run smoothly.

So are you and I "modern" people just because we live in a world that is filled with gleaming machines? In Noah Webster's dictionary, he tells us that "modern" means something that is "pertaining to the present time, or time not long past." So perhaps the idea of the modern world actually has a lot to do with time and history. Perhaps we are modern because of all that has gone before.

Historians say that the modern world really began in the eighteenth century, when people began using steam engines and coal-fired furnaces. Railroad tracks were built, crisscrossing the countrysides, and suddenly people could move about much more quickly. They were no longer tied to their little villages, walking or riding on horseback when they wished to go somewhere. Large factories powered by steam and coal arose, and workers streamed into the cities to work in the factories, leaving the farms in the country behind. The cities grew larger, with many new needs, and more inventions appeared to solve those problems. As the nineteenth century progressed, the telephone, electric lights, the automobile, the airplane, and the refrigerator were created, all to help cities and businesses run more smoothly and make life easier for the many people living there.

Every time a scientist or an inventor devised something new, other scientists learned from it and built upon it. The pace of scientific learning grew faster, and the inventions came along at a greater and greater rate, because each new breakthrough created the opportunity for dozens more. And the news of these discoveries was flashed around the world more quickly than ever before in history, because now it was possible for a man living in Paris, France, to pick up a newspaper and read about something that had happened in New York City just a few days before. The modern world became a smaller place, because telephones and telegraphs, television and radio made it so.

As the cities grew larger, and the inventions more wondrous, the nations grew more wealthy and powerful, and more determined to keep and perhaps even expand their power. Instead of kings, most countries came to be ruled by presidents and prime ministers, and also dictators. Some of these leaders were good and wise, but some were terrible, eager to spread their evil beyond the borders of their own nations. From their actions, the smoke of war would arise to shadow the life of every person on earth.

We are modern people because we live in a world filled with cities, where science rushes forward and new inventions appear every year. Our world is small because we can know at the touch of a computer key what is happening anywhere on the globe and then talk about it with friends next door and far away. We live in powerful nations who guard their influence and mastery jealously, and who seek ever greater wealth by buying and selling continuously with one another, so that what happens in one of these nations affects all of the others. We are modern because of the history that went before us.

In this book, I will tell you stories of the modern nations, from the nineteenth and twentieth centuries. These are stories of great things: of science and exploration, of perseverance and courage. But these are also stories of war and conflict, and the grasping desire for power. This is the modern world: are you ready to hear its tales? Then turn to the next page with me, and let us begin!

Chapter 2

How Bismarck Made an Empire
by Charles Morris

In the year 1800 there was a German people, but no German nation. There was only a collection of little kingdoms, each with its own proud prince. If you were to fling down a pane of glass, splintering it into many fragments—some large, some medium sized, and some small,—so Germany seemed to have been thrown down on the map of Europe and splintered into bits. In the south was one great piece called the Empire of Austria. In the north was another piece not so large called the Kingdom of Prussia. Then there were medium pieces called Saxony and Bavaria. After them came smaller pieces, and then a large number of tiny bits, some of them not much larger than a corn farm in Nebraska. There were more than three hundred of these states, some of which looked as if you might pick them up and put them in your pocket. They had their rulers, and their capitals, and their armies—if you call that an army which is made up of a drummer, a general, and a dozen or two men.

For many centuries these German states had been joined together in what was called the "Holy Roman Empire of the German Nation." They pretended to keep up the old Empire of Rome, but in truth they were like so many beads on a string. Do you remember learning of the great conqueror Napoleon? He cut the string and away went the beads: he put an end to the Holy Roman Empire. He joined many of the small states together and gave some of the little ones to the large ones, so that when he got through, instead of more than three hundred, there were only thirty-nine.

Two of these, Austria and Prussia, were powerful nations. In the year 1862, the king of Prussia died and a new king came to the throne, under the name of Wilhelm I. One of the first things King Wilhelm did was to choose for his minister the ablest man in Germany, Count Otto von Bismarck. Now this Bismarck was very much like Cardinal Richelieu in France, about whom you may have read. You might remember that Richelieu was the true power in France, and made King Louis great. In Prussia, it was Count Bismarck who stood behind the throne and held all the power, and if it had not been for him, history would have very little to say about the great Emperor Wilhelm of Germany. It was Bismarck who made a big emperor out of a little king.

Bismarck was a very able man, but he was also a tyrant. When he said yes, King Wilhelm never said no. He made laws without asking the parliament. He laid taxes, formed treaties with foreign nations, and did everything very much as he pleased. And what he was most pleased to do was to make Prussia powerful, the most powerful nation in Europe.

So Prussia began to drill soldiers, and collect guns and powder and shot, and invent new weapons of war, until its army got to be the strongest in Europe. Then Prussia went to war with Denmark and took a large piece of land from that little kingdom. A short while later, a dispute arose between Prussia and Austria, and at once Bismarck declared war. It was one of the shortest wars in history. In a few weeks, Austria was completely beaten, and Prussia became the great power in Germany.

Now we must shift our eyes away from Prussia for just a moment and look over toward France. Do you remember learning about Louis Napoleon? You have probably read about the blunder that Napoleon made when he tried to start an empire in Mexico, and how quickly he got out when the United States told him to go. This blunder made him very unpopular indeed with his own people, and he began to fear that they would topple him off his throne.

There was one way to put them in good humor again, and that was to go to war and win great victories. Thoughtfully, his eye turned toward Germany. If he could only defeat the Prussians, who had defeated the Austrians, it would make him a greater man than ever. Louis Napoleon thought he had a very fine army, and he had a new kind of gun which could throw twenty-five musket balls at once. He fancied that with his soldiers and his machine gun he could make as short work with Prussia as that country had done with Austria. As for the thousands of men who would be killed and wounded, and the families which would be ruined and thrown into misery and despair by a war, that did not seem to trouble him. He thought a great deal more of himself and his power than of the people of France and Germany.

Of course, I am talking here about something that I only guess at. We do not often know the secret thoughts in the brains of kings and emperors, and can judge of what they think only by what they do. What Louis Napoleon seemed to do was to look around him for some excuse for a war, something to fight about. What reason could he find to start a war with Prussia? He found one in Spain, which just then had no king and which had offered its throne to a cousin of the royal family of Prussia, named Leopold. He accepted it, as was very natural, since such an offer does not often present itself.

For Louis Napoleon, here was an excuse for war, ready-made: he did not want to see a Prussian on the Spanish throne. He sent word to King Wilhelm of Prussia that he must not let Prince Leopold accept the crown of Spain. King Wilhelm sent word back that he had nothing to do with it, and that Leopold was his own master and free to do what he pleased. When Leopold heard of all this uproar he drew back and said he would not have the throne of Spain. That ought to have ended the whole business, and it would, if Napoleon had not wanted a war. As it was, he wrote to King Wilhelm that it was not right to let Leopold accept the throne without consulting him and his cabinet. King Wilhelm replied that he had nothing more to say, and that he would not stop Prince Leopold from doing what he pleased in the matter. That was enough. Napoleon had found the excuse he wanted. He at once declared war against Prussia.

I have used the name of King Wilhelm, but the fact is that those answers came from Count Bismarck. The king danced when Bismarck played the fiddle. And when the war began, it was not the king who fought it, but a great general named Helmuth von Moltke, who could handle an army better than any man in Europe. As for the emperor Louis Napoleon, he blindly went to war without knowing what he was about. His uncle, the great Napoleon, knew all about his army; the little Napoleon knew nothing about his. The war minister told him that all was ready, and that "not a single button was wanting on a single gaiter." In fact, nothing was ready, and there was a good deal more wanting than gaiter buttons. It was only in the Prussian army that everything was ready and not a button was missing.

The French were as ignorant of the state of affairs as the emperor. "On to Berlin!" they shouted, flinging their hats into the air. They were full of high spirits. They said that in a few days they would be across the borders, and in a few weeks they would be in the Prussian capital, and then King Wilhelm and Count Bismarck would be glad to beg for peace. But in fact they did not cross the border at all, they did not set foot on German territory, and the German army marched into Paris instead of the French army into Berlin.

When the French army reached the frontier, what did they see? There was the German army ready to meet them, moving like clockwork, every wheel of it fitting neatly into another wheel.

General Moltke was too old to march at the head of the army, but he laid out all the plans so finely that it was said he had only to strike a bell and everything went as he wished. That was not the way with the French. There was no clockwork about their army. They were brave enough, but they had no great leader, no fine organization, no large supplies, and there was confusion in all their movements. They had gone to war blindly and would soon pay the price.

Louis Napoleon marched with his army, his heart full of pride and hope. The telegraph lines were all ready to carry back the news of his victories to Paris. King Wilhelm was with his army, too, quite as confident, and with more reason. The two armies met on August 2, 1870, and within a week four battles had been fought. In the first the French met with a little success, and the wires took to Paris the story of a brilliant victory. After that they had nothing but the tale of defeat to carry.

On August 6th there was a terrible battle at a place called Worth. It lasted fifteen hours, and the French were defeated and had to retreat. But they had not gone far before the Germans were ahead of them, cutting them off. Then two more battles were fought. On August 16th the two armies met at a place called Gravelotte, the Germans with 200,000 men, the French with 140,000. Here was fought the greatest battle of the war. The armies struggled face-to-face all day long. Both sides were brave and resolute. The French held their ground and died like heroes. The Germans dashed on them and died like heroes. For nine hours the terrible conflict went on, and 40,000 men fell dead or wounded on the bloody field. Then the French general gave it up and withdrew his men to the strong city of Metz. He had fought bravely but had failed. The Germans surrounded Metz and held him there. In this way half the French army was shut up in a cage.

There was another army, about 140,000 men, that was with Louis Napoleon. They tried to reach Metz and help their fellow French soldiers, but Moltke laid his plans to stop them. He drove the French back, and at the end of August they gathered around a fortress named Sedan, on the Belgian frontier of France. It was just the sort of place Moltke wanted to get them in. He laughed when he saw them there. "The trap is closed and the mouse in it," he said.

The German army spread out till they surrounded the French, and poured on them such a hailstorm of shot and shell that the valley was filled with dead and wounded. The French fought with their old courage, but they could not get out, and they were killed in multitudes. In the end the whole army had to surrender. On the 2nd of September, just one month after the first fight, an army of 83,000 men became prisoners of war, and with them was Louis Napoleon.

Two days afterwards Louis Napoleon ceased to be emperor. A meeting was held in Paris, a new government was formed, the emperor was deposed, and a republic was established. This was a revolution, though it was finished in a day and without a shot being fired or a drop of blood shed. There have not been many revolutions like that.

The war went on, but France had no chance to win. On October 30th the French army in Metz surrendered. Then the Germans gathered around Paris and besieged that great city. Here the French made their last strong fight. They held out for four months, until the people were so hungry that they had to eat the animals in the zoological garden. They gave up when there was nothing more to eat. Soon all the armies of France were dispersed, all its fortresses were captured, and the Germans were masters of France. Louis Napoleon's war had proved the greatest blunder of his life, for it ruined his country and ended his reign.

There is one more thing of great importance to speak about— "How Bismarck made an Empire." What that great statesman wished to do was to restore the old German Empire and put Prussia at its head. This he had long worked for; now the time had come to finish his task. North Germany was united with Prussia; he got the South German states to enter into the same union, and to form an empire with King Wilhelm at its head.

His great work was finished at Versailles, the royal city of France, on the 18th of January, 1871. It was done with the utmost splendor and show, and when the crown of the empire was put on the head of the new emperor, Wilhelm I of Germany, there was such a shout as had seldom been heard there before, and the whole great assembly sang the national hymns of Germany. The country of the Germans was divided into the German Empire and the Austrian Empire, and the emperor of Germany was one of the leading monarchs of Europe. To Count Bismarck he owed his power and his fame.

All of Europe was changed now. Germany was powerful and intended to stay that way by whatever means it could. What shall come of Germany's ambitions and thirst for power? A great sorrow, as you shall see in the chapters to come.

Chapter 3

How China Opened Its Doors
by Charles Morris

I think there are times when all of us are tired of learning new things and want to be let alone with the knowledge we already have. That is the way it was with China. During the 1800s, many of the world's nations were drawing ever closer to each other, through trade and art and books, and also through war and fighting, as we have seen in the story of Prussia and France's Louis Napoleon. But the Chinese were proud of their old ways, their old books, their old religions and government and laws, and thought that all the rest of the world had nothing half so good. After all, China had been an old and established kingdom long before the nations of Europe and America had even been conceived. They were mere children beside China. The idea of these young upstarts coming to teach new things to a gray-haired nation which had been rich in learning thousands of years before they were born! Such a thing was too ridiculous to be thought of. That is the way China looked at it, and that is the reason it did not open its arms to the civilization of the West. Its people were proud and self-satisfied.

But even so, China could not keep out the West and its ways.

England was the first of the Western nations to get into China. The British wanted trade, a very bad kind of trade, for English ships carried opium to China. Opium is a dangerous drug, made from the lovely red blossoms of poppies. It causes the people who smoke it to lose their senses. Many Chinese people became slaves to this terrible drug, willing to commit any crime in order to buy more of it from the British traders, whose ships were anchored in the port of Canton, their holds stuffed with bundles of opium. The emperor of China did not like this; he was horrified by the changes that he saw in his people, and he knew that opium was the cause of much sorrow. So he gave orders that all the opium in Canton should be seized and destroyed, and $20 million worth of the drug was thrown overboard into the dark water.

This made the English furious. The trade in opium was a very profitable enterprise, and they did not want to lose it! They sent their warships to China and began what is called the Opium War. England was in the wrong, of course, to attack another country over so shameful a thing; but in war the wrong often prevails, if it has the best guns. China was defeated, and was forced to open five of its ports to the world's commerce, and give up to England the large city and fine port of Hong Kong.

This was the first step in the opening of China. Twenty years afterwards another war broke out, in which the British and the French joined. In 1860 they marched to Peking, the capital of China, commanded it to open its gates, and burned the emperor's summer palace, one of the finest buildings in the whole land. Once again, China was forced to accept more of the foreigner's demands. More of China was revealed to the world, more ships were allowed to dock in China's ports, more of the world's trade goods were allowed to be sold in China's markets. In this way the door of China was opened; a little at a time; now a small crack and now a larger crack.

Little by little, foreign things crept in. In 1876 a railroad was built, just a few miles long. The emperor did not like it, but now he was afraid to deal with it as strongly as he had with the opium. He took a safer plan; he bought the railroad with China's own gold, and then tore up the rails and stored them away. But he could not stop the flood that was coming. The next year a telegraph line was built. This time he could not buy it, and he could not destroy it. Before long, many miles of telegraph wires were crisscrossing China.

There are some nations which nothing but the boom of the cannon and the crack of the rifle can rouse from their long sleep, and China was one of them. In 1894 China entered into a war that I may call a "great awakening," for it gave the sleeping empire a very hard shake. This war was with Japan, that small island nation separated from China by a thin stretch of ocean called the Sea of Japan. Unlike China, Japan had thrown wide its doors and eagerly accepted the new ideas and methods of the Western nations, and had built up its army with new tactics and fearsome new weapons. Japan was ready for war, and China was not.

This war came out of a quarrel over a nearby kingdom called Korea. It occupied a large peninsula directly between China and Japan, and its rulers were weak and squabbling. It presented an easy target for both China and Japan, and both of them wanted it. Korea was like a bone being fought over by two dogs.

Now, China was like a great mastiff and Japan like a small-sized bulldog. No doubt, the rulers of China thought they would make short work of this impudent little island empire. They might have done so forty years before, but now Japan had an army of well-drilled and well-armed soldiers, trained in the newest ideas, and it made short work of the sleepy colossus. The bulldog got its teeth in the throat of the mastiff and soon shook all the fight out of it. In a very short time little Japan had whipped big China; it might have tried to swallow it if it had not been so very large.

What a shock for China! How could this have happened? How could they have been beaten by a nation so very much smaller than they? It was as if the very smallest boy in a classroom had faced down the biggest bully and forced him to run away! Slowly, a new notion seems to have come into the great brain of China. It had been thoroughly whipped by a little nation of its own kind. It was clear enough that it had a good deal to learn, and that it must give up some of its stubborn pride. Perhaps the outside world of the foreigners had something to teach, after all.

This lesson was not lost on China. Railroads were no longer forbidden; they began to make their way through the "Celestial Kingdom." Steamboats plowed the waters for a thousand miles up the great Yangtze River. Foreign engineers began to work the rich coal and iron mines. Factories sprang up in the foreign settlements, with the best modern machinery. Foreign books were translated and read. Missionaries taught the people in hundreds of places. The ambassadors of the nations were admitted to Peking and received in open audience by the emperor. China was giving way to the eager pressure of the Western world.

But it was only the high government officials of China who saw the benefit of this. The great masses of the people were full of ignorance and prejudice, and they hated the Western people bitterly. The best name they had for them was "foreign devils." Suddenly, in the year 1900, there came an uprising. A secret society of the people, who were called the Boxers, began murdering foreign people wherever they could find them. They entered Peking in multitudes, and many of the soldiers in the Chinese army joined them in a bloodthirsty attack on the embassies and representatives of the foreign nations. Never had such a thing happened before, and the nations of the world sent soldiers to China to prevent this terrible crime. This army marched to Peking and rescued the ambassadors and other foreigners, but they had to fight the Boxer army every step of the way to get there, and the old nation was stirred up as never before. The emperor's court was fiercely divided between those officials who wished to side with the Boxers and throw all foreigners out of China, and those who believed the Boxers were acting wrongly and must be stopped.

The foreign army was victorious, and the Boxer Rebellion was stopped, but the divided heart of China continued to war with itself. Accept foreign ways or oppose them? Draw closer to the rest of the world or turn away?

In 1908 the emperor died. He had been a member of the Qing dynasty, which had led China since the days of the great king Kangxi, whom you may remember. The Qing family was no longer great, though, and when the emperor's brother tried to take the throne and rule China, he was unable to succeed. Loud voices throughout China complained bitterly against him, and against the Qing, who had allowed China to be so bitterly defeated by a foreign army. China must be strong again, they cried. China must turn in a new direction!

And so it did. A new leader arose, a man named Sun Yat-sen, who led his followers in an uprising that forced the emperor Puyi to step down off his throne, the last ruler of the Qing Dynasty, the last emperor of China. China was declared to be a republic, and Sun Yat-sen was elected its first president in December of 1911.

In this way did China enter the modern world.

Chapter 4

Sailing through the Sand

Have any of you ever wished that you could ride a camel? Imagine clambering aboard one of those grumpy beasts and setting off across the sands of the Sinai Peninsula, that great triangle of desert that stretches from the Mediterranean Sea down to the Red Sea. You might be gently humping along, seeing nothing for miles around but rocky outcrops and sandy dunes, pretending to be Moses leading the Israelites out of Egypt, when suddenly, you pull your camel to a stop and rub your eyes disbelievingly. What is it that you are seeing? For there ahead of you is a giant ship, an oil tanker, gliding serenely through the desert dunes! How can this be? Quickly you send your camel shambling forward again, and, as you climb the last dune, you see the answer to this riddle: the ship is sailing in a huge canal, which stretches to the north and south as far as you can see. Beyond the far bank, the land of Egypt spreads in all its ancient glory, and you can see settlements and the green of palm trees along the canal's Egyptian shore. The huge oil tanker sails on, and, as you look to the south, you can see another coming, and another behind that one, a line of ships moving ever northward to the Mediterranean.

The dream of ships sailing through the desert is not a new one. In ancient times, the pharaohs of Egypt looked thoughtfully at the narrow neck of land that separated the Nile River from the Red Sea. It was only sixty miles, and there were several lakes along the way. What if the river could be connected to the lakes, and the lakes to the Sea? First one pharaoh and then another, over the course of hundreds of years, sent slaves and workers to dig. Sometimes they were successful, and the resulting canal would be used for many years, but always, in the end, the desert would overcome the will of man, filling the canal with its shifting sands and making travel through it impossible again. Men continued to try, though. When the Persian emperor Darius conquered Egypt, one of the first things he did was order his workmen to dig out the canal. When Rome ruled Egypt, her warships sailed the canal. And 1,000 years later, when the French conqueror Napoleon gained control of Egypt, can you guess what one of his purposes there might be? Oh yes, the canal! In 1799 he sent his surveyors out to determine the exact site of the ancient waterway. He dreamed of ships sailing easily from Europe to Asia through a French canal, and of all the money he would collect from them in payment for such passage! But his scientists told him that the project was impossible, and so, reluctantly, he did not pursue it.

Still the dream did not die. In 1832 it captured the imagination of a young Frenchman named Ferdinand de Lessops.

Ferdinand was an engineer, which is a special kind of builder who figures out how to construct something so that it works for a certain purpose. In 1832, he was living in Cairo, Egypt, working as a representative of the French government. One day, idly searching for something to read, he opened up a package of books that had been sent to him by a friend. Inside he found a report written by one of Napoleon's surveyors, telling the story of the ancient canal and the traces of it that the surveyors had found.

Ferdinand was transfixed by this idea. A canal through the desert! He grew more excited as he thought about it. What if this canal could connect the Red Sea, not with the Nile River, but with the Mediterranean? Quickly, he checked his maps and performed some calculations. Yes, the distance was only one hundred miles. Surely it could be done! Such a canal would save immense amounts of time and cost, because ships would no longer have to sail all the way around the tip of Africa to go back and forth between Europe and Asia. A trip through the canal would spare them almost six thousand miles of sailing!

A great desire filled the heart of Ferdinand de Lessops: he wanted to build this canal. But life's demands and the requirements of his job with the French government filled his time. For the next twenty years, however much the canal may have occupied his thoughts, Ferdinand was obliged to keep his plans to himself. He was posted to different spots all across the globe and did not return to Egypt until 1854.

In that year, the land of the pharaohs was under the rule of the Ottoman Turks, about whom you have, no doubt, read. But the Turks had little interest in truly ruling there and had instead appointed a viceroy, or substitute ruler, named Mohammed Said. Now, this Said happened to be a very old friend of Ferdinand de Lessops. When Ferdinand heard that Said was now ruler of Egypt, he traveled there immediately and presented his friend with his plan for a canal. Said approved of it at once, but he told Ferdinand that he could not begin to build until he also received permission from the Ottoman Sultan. And, he said, you will have to find a way to pay for it!

These were both rather difficult problems for Ferdinand to solve. The Ottoman Sultan was not disposed to look upon the canal with a friendly eye. And building the canal would be very expensive indeed.

Reasoning that he could do nothing to influence the mind of a Sultan so far away, Ferdinand concentrated on the money problem. He decided to sell shares in the canal; this means that, for a certain amount of money, any person could buy a tiny portion of the canal. Then, from the profits that the canal would make by charging a toll for every ship that passed through it, the people who had bought shares would be paid back both what they had spent and a little extra. Ferdinand went throughout France selling shares, persuading his countrymen that building this canal would only increase the glory of France. It was the patriotic duty of every Frenchmen to support it, he cried. Many of them agreed, and about half of the shares in the canal were bought by the people of France.

At this point, Ferdinand had $20 million. I know that that sounds like a great deal of money, but it was actually only half of what he needed. Nevertheless, and without waiting any longer to get permission from the Sultan, Ferdinand began to dig. Like the ancient pharaohs and King Darius, Ferdinand went to battle against the desert sand.

A strip of land separating two bodies of water is called an isthmus, and the particular strip of land that Ferdinand was attacking is called the Isthmus of Suez. If you look for it on a globe, you will see, with Egypt on one side and the Sinai desert on the other, a tiny sliver of land, a fragile splinter between the huge Mediterranean and the questing finger of the Red Sea. It does not look like much of anything at all, compared to the immensity of the globe: a mere one hundred miles of sand. But now you must imagine one hundred miles of sand, where each bucketful must be moved by hand and a huge trench dug, big enough to float an ocean-going ship. That was the challenge that Ferdinand was facing.

He saw at once that he must find every possible shortcut. Like the pharaohs before him, he planned to take advantage of the lakes along the way; there are five of them, in a rough line north to south. Ferdinand decided that he would connect those five lakes to each other, and then dig the canal outwards both ways to join with the Seas on either end. The lakes would also provide a place for ships to pass each other, so that traffic on the canal could go both ways, but the canal itself would only have to be wide enough for one ship at a time. Still, even using the lakes, the workers would have to move one hundred million tons of sand.

Wielding his own pickaxe, on a hot spring morning in 1859,

Ferdinand led a little crowd of 150 workers to the edge of the first lake, Lake Manzala. A ragged cheer went up as Ferdinand swung his axe and dug the first bucketful of sand from the damp lake shore. Then he turned to the workmen, and they too began to dig. It was very slow at first. The workmen had to scoop mud up from the bottom of the lake and pile it along the edges of the trench that they were building. The mud dried as hard as cement in the fierce desert sun and made the edges of the canal sturdy enough to use as roads. Throughout the next few years, the laborers continued to dig the canal by hand, as Ferdinand traveled throughout Europe, trying to sell more shares. Finally, by 1864, he had enough money to buy machinery to help with the digging, and the work began to go more quickly. The giant digging machines helped Ferdinand to finally defeat the desert's shifting sands.

Up at the northern end of the canal, on the Mediterranean Sea, a town was springing up. It was named Port Said, after the viceroy of Egypt. Workers there were building a harbor, making the sea floor deeper so that ships could dock before beginning their journey down the canal. As the canal grew, other towns and settlements began to blossom along its banks, and gardens and orchards were planted. Animals began to arrive, making their homes along the water where before only barren sand had whispered.

After ten years, the Suez Canal was complete. It opened in November 1869: 100 miles long, 175 feet wide, and 26 feet deep, big enough for a large ship. By using the canal, and the Transcontinental Railroad that had been completed in the United States six months earlier, a traveler could circle the entire world faster than had ever before been possible. Ships of all nations began to use the canal at once, and world travel has been forever changed by its construction. Today it is even bigger: it is 985 feet wide, and more than 60 feet deep.

In Port Said, for many years after the canal was opened, a granite statue of Ferdinand de Lessops stood near its northern mouth. The stony eyes looked ever onward as the ships sailed through the sand and out into the Mediterranean. At the statue's base were carved these words: "To open the world to all people." That was Ferdinand de Lessop's dream, and it was fulfilled.

Chapter 5

A Tower of Air and Iron

In 1864, when the Suez Canal was opened, a young Frenchman named Gustave journeyed all the way from Paris to study it. Gustave, you see, was a builder, an engineer just like Ferdinand de Lessops. An engineer must think of all the different ways that his creation could be used, all the different problems that it might encounter, and then build it so that it meets every challenge. Being an engineer is like being a solver of puzzles.

As Gustave studied the canal that day, he was especially interested in its metalwork, for he loved to build with metal. He had only recently built an iron railway bridge over the Garonne, one of France's most turbulent rivers. Building bridges was a dangerous occupation, and building with iron was even more so, because, in 1864, iron was still a fairly new material to work with. While building his giant bridge, Gustave had needed to invent new ways to curve and brace the iron, so that it would support the heavy burden of the bridge's weight. Gustave had planned every aspect of his bridge, making many drawings and plans. In fact, Gustave had planned the bridge so carefully that the only problem that arose during the whole time he was building it was that one worker became careless, and slipped and fell into the wild Garonne River. Gustave himself had been obliged to carefully remove his coat and shoes, and then dive in to rescue his man!

The placid surface of the Suez Canal was nothing like the

crashing waves of the river. But both the canal and the river had been conquered by metal, and Gustave knew that iron would be able to conquer even greater challenges!

So he left Egypt and returned to his office in Paris. He thought about iron all the time—new ways to make arches and supports, and girders and columns, so that his iron structures could be taller and broader and bigger. As Gustave's skill with iron grew, he was hired for larger, complicated projects: huge railway bridges, giant iron skeletons for train stations and churches. Soon Gustave and his iron beams could be found in almost any corner of the world, solving construction problems that had never been tackled before.

For instance, in 1879 a French railroad company asked Gustave to build a huge, arched bridge over a canyon four hundred feet deep. The finished bridge would be almost two thousand feet long: the highest and longest bridge in the world! Gustave accepted this challenge, and he sat in his office for many days, thinking about iron and also thinking about wind. Gustave had good reason to be concerned about wind. Let me tell you why.

Just a year before, in 1878, a great iron bridge had been built in Scotland, not by Gustave but by an Englishman named Thomas Bouch. It was called the Tay Bridge, and the newspapers called it "a marvel of the ages." But Mr. Bouch had not properly considered the wind. I wonder if you have ever thought about it? I am sure that you have stood outside on a blustery day and felt the force of the wind in a particularly strong gust. You can understand, then, that the bigger a thing may be, the stronger the wind will push against it. Can you imagine the force of the wind pushing against a giant iron bridge? But Mr. Bouch had not imagined it, not correctly. And so, one night, a mighty storm blew up, and the Tay Bridge collapsed, just when a train was crossing it, and everyone on board that train was killed.

Gustave was determined never to make such a mistake. For the rest of his life, he thought about wind almost as much as he thought about iron.

And so he planned most carefully for his giant canyon bridge. He tested the iron to see how it would act both in the hot summer sun and the freezing gales of winter. He visited the foundry, which is the place where iron is created from melted ore, and inspected each piece of the bridge as it was made. Again he made hundreds of drawings and planned the arch so that it would be as sturdy as possible. Because the canyon was so deep, he had to build the arch in two parts, one from each side. Gustave's plans were so precise that the two sides of the arch met in the middle perfectly, without even an inch of error.

It took Gustave five years to build the canyon bridge. When it was done, other engineers went to admire it, just as Gustave had done that day long ago along the Suez Canal, and they said to one another, "Surely this is Gustave's finest work."

But was it? You must be the judge, for I will tell you what Gustave did next.

One day, when Gustave was back in his office in Paris, he received a letter from one of France's best-known artists, a sculptor named Frederic-Auguste Bartholdi. Bartholdi had a problem: he had been hired by the government of France to create a beautiful and noble statue of a woman standing tall, with a crown upon her head and a torch in her raised hand. She was to be called Lady Liberty, and she was to be sent to the United States of America as a gift from the people of France.

Bartholdi had no difficulty in planning just how she should look, but how was he to construct this giant lady so that she could be taken apart, put aboard a ship, sent across the ocean, and put back together again in New York City? "I have heard you are a good solver of problems," he wrote to Gustave. "Can you help?"

As he sat holding the letter, Gustave thought of another problem, too. Can you think what it might be? Wind, of course! The statue was meant to stand in New York Harbor, and so she must withstand the fierce winds that might blow in off the Atlantic Ocean.

As always, Gustave accepted the challenge. He decided that the solution to all of the problems facing Lady Liberty would be to build for her an enormous iron skeleton and attach giant sheets of copper for her skin. The skeleton's beams would then be sunk deep into the statue's stone base. That should make her sturdy enough to weather anything, even an Atlantic hurricane, Gustave reasoned. And she would also be light enough to travel by ship to her new home.

In 1883 hundreds of Parisians gathered to watch as Gustave's workmen hammered 300 sheets of copper to the statue's iron bones. When they were done, gasps of admiration filled the street. There stood Bartholdi's graceful Lady, proudly lifting her torch. Gustave's idea had worked perfectly. The statue was taken apart in Paris, with all her pieces numbered; placed aboard a ship for her ride to her new home; and put back together again atop Liberty Island in New York Harbor. I wonder how many of my readers have been there to visit her? Now you know the man who made it possible for you to do so!

Again the engineers of France shook their heads in wonder. "You are amazing, Gustave! This is your most impressive work!"

But was it? You shall judge!

In 1887, just a few years later, Gustave received another letter in the mail. This time, it was an invitation to join a competition: a Committee would choose a builder to construct a tower one thousand feet high, taller than any tower the world had ever seen.

Who would want such a tower? Why, it was the city of Paris itself, and they wanted it for the glory of France. You see, in just two years, in 1889, Paris was to be the host city for a World's Fair, which is a great gathering of representatives from all nations to show examples of each nation's industry and greatness. The city of Paris was determined that all the nations who came to the fair must be in awe of the magnificence of France.

But how to do this? Why, what could be more grand than a tower one thousand feet tall!

What a challenge! No one had every built a tower so high. The tallest structure in the world at that time was the Washington Memorial in the United States, and it was only 550 feet tall. But Gustave was certain he could do it. And, he said, he would build it out of iron! Not stone or wood; men had been building with those things for thousands of years. Iron was new and wonderful; what better way to show the world the future of France than with a tower of iron! Gustave displayed his plans to the Committee: an iron tower with gracefully arched legs built in a lacy, latticework pattern.

"It looks like it is floating!" one of the men exclaimed, looking at the drawings. Gustave smiled. His tower did look light and airy, but he did not take the trouble to explain to the Committee that the reason for this was . . . wind! Gustave's lacy design would allow the wind to blow right through the tower.

Out of the hundreds of ideas that they received, the Committee chose Gustave's. But, they said to him, there is just one little problem. We do not actually have the money to build this tower. You must come up with that yourself.

Gustave agreed. He would build the great tower with his own money, but he made the city of Paris promise that the tower would belong to him alone for the next twenty years.

"I wish to have it to myself," he said. "I wish to conduct experiments upon the wind from the tower's top!"

Gustave began to build. He sunk huge blocks of stone into the ground and angled them to anchor the gracefully arching legs of the tower. Then piece by piece, Gustave's workmen began to bolt the iron beams together. They matched each piece to one of the 1,800 diagrams that Gustave and his artists had drawn for this project, to be certain that every bolt and every beam was perfectly in line with all the rest. Slowly, slowly the tower rose, higher and higher, until it began to be visible from rooftops all across Paris.

Suddenly, an outcry arose. A group of artists and writers sent an angry letter to the Committee. "What is this monstrosity? This ugly chimney of iron! Why, it looks like the skeleton of something else—it is a disgrace!"

"He is already building it, and he will own it for the next twenty years," the Committee replied stiffly. "You must either learn to like it, or leave Paris!"

Gustave didn't think his tower was a monster. He thought it beautiful, and, in its way, a giant exclamation point of triumph—the triumph of iron.

When the World's Fair opened in 1889, Gustave's creation towered over the entranceway to the exhibition grounds. People clamored to ascend into it: the tower had three platforms, each higher than the next, all connected with a new and wonderful invention, the elevator. For a small price, a visitor could visit the first platform, with its cafes and shops; for a larger price, the second platform; and for a still larger price, the third platform, with its amazing view of Paris, a view that until then had only been seen by birds.

Visitors to the third platform noticed a small spiral staircase, leading upward to yet a fourth platform, high above. Can we ascend there as well? they asked eagerly. Oh no, they were told. That leads to the private apartment of Monsieur Eiffel. He lives up there and conducts experiments upon the wind.

Monsieur Eiffel? Who might that be? I am sure that you have guessed that the builder of this great tower was our friend Gustave Eiffel, and now you know that he should be acclaimed for far greater deeds than merely building the tower that bears his name!

Chapter 6

The Boer War
by Charles Morris

I wonder if my readers remember the word Boer. It referred
to the Dutch and French peasants who settled in South
Africa but rebelled in 1840 when the English tried to rule them.
They let the English have their Cape Colony in South Africa and
forged a new land and new government of their own further north.
In their two new Boer republics, the Orange River Free State and
the Transvaal Republic, the Boers thought they were now free
from the English, but in that they made a great mistake. Every
year the English were getting nearer, and at length a remarkable
thing took place: diamonds were found in the country west of the
Boer republics.

You know how a magnet draws iron. In much the same way
diamonds and gold draw men. English diamond hunters came in
multitudes and began digging for the shining stones. The Boers
did not like these neighbors, and the Africans did not like them
any better. A warlike tribe of natives, called the Zulus, began
fighting with the English and were easily beaten back. Then in
1877, the English made an excuse to march into the Transvaal and
claim it for their own.

You may be sure the bold Boers were angry at this. They
hated the English and did not like being governed and taxed by

them, but they bore it all with stern and sullen faces until the year 1880. Then they seized their well-tried muskets, gathered into companies, and decided to drive the strangers from their land. Everywhere that they met the English, they defeated them. At a place called Majuba Hill, they gave them a terrible beating that ended the war. The English were driven out of the country, and for a time the Boers had peace.

The diamonds had caused trouble enough, but not long afterwards an even stronger and more dangerous magnet was found. Gold was discovered, large veins of it, not outside, but inside the Transvaal Republic. Mines were dug and in time they proved to be the richest in the world. Miners came from all corners of the globe, and of course many came from England too. They settled in the Transvaal, where they built a great miner's city named Johannesburg. It grew until it had more than 100,000 inhabitants.

If you have read the history of gold, you know that nothing in all the ages has made so much trouble for mankind. The poor Boers soon found that their gold was a curse. The strangers in Johannesburg said that, as they lived in the country and paid taxes there, they ought to have some say in its government. This the Boers did not want to give them, for they were so many that they would soon outvote them and get possession of their land by the aid of ballots instead of bullets. So Paul Kruger, the Boer president, said that the miners could not become citizens until they had lived there for many years.

After that trouble came swiftly. An ambitious man named Cecil Rhodes had become chief owner of the diamond mines and had conquered the country north of the Transvaal. Then in 1895, he sent a party of men down to stir up a rebellion in Johannesburg and help the gold miners to take possession of the Boers' country. In this he had miscalculated, though. The men who had fought at Majuba Hill were still alive, and after a short, swift battle they took all of Cecil Rhodes' men prisoners and locked them up in jail.

Again, the Boers had avoided catastrophe, but not for long.

In 1899, new trouble came, all through that pestilent gold. The gold miners in Johannesburg said that they were oppressed by Paul Kruger and his government, and demanded the right to help make the laws under which they lived. The British government joined the dispute and commanded the Boers to give the miners some rights in the country. The Boers fiercely disagreed and demanded of the British government what right it had to interfere in Boer affairs! Every day the dispute grew hotter. Both sides were preparing for war, and British soldiers were put on ships that were sailing for South Africa. Paul Kruger said this was completely unacceptable, and he gave Great Britain just one day to order its soldiers back. But no attention was paid to his words, and so he declared war on England.

Likely enough this is just what the government of Great Britain wanted. Perhaps they thought they would make short work of the Transvaal and sweep it off the map of the world. But they did not find this to be quite so easy a task. The people of the two Boer republics joined their forces and sent their soldiers into England's colonies on the east side of Africa, and its Cape Colony on the west. Wherever the Boers met the British they drove them back, and soon had them shut up inside three towns: Ladysmith, Kimberley, and Mafeking.

The British tried to drive the Boers away from those towns, but they could not. The Boer armies encircled the towns and besieged them for months. Whenever the armies met in open battle, the British were defeated. This Boer War was not the trifling little job the English had calculated on. So England woke up and saw that it had a big war indeed on its hands. Men and horses and cannon and guns were brought in from all sides, an overwhelming gathering of British might. Money was spent like water; English colonies in Canada and Australia sent troops to Africa; Lord Roberts, the best general Great Britain had, was put in command. The ocean swarmed with ships carrying men and supplies to the south, toward Africa.

The Boers were overwhelmed. The countryside seemed alive with British soldiers. The Boers fought bravely still, but step by step they were forced to retreat. They gave up the sieges on the three towns. The Orange River Free State was overrun by English troops. Then Johannesburg, the city of gold, and Pretoria, the Boer capital, were occupied. The Boer army broke up. Little bands of Boer soldiers tried to continue to attack and defend, but the case now was hopeless. The few scattered Boers could not stand against the mighty British army. The Boer republics were at an end. They were soon to be swept into the great net of the British empire, and Cape Colony was destined to spread until it covered almost all of South Africa. Great Britain had become the greatest power in Africa.

Chapter 7

Discoveries in the Sea of Ice
by Charles Morris

If any of my young readers, in the pursuit of knowledge, should enter a public library and go to the shelves devoted to books of travel and discovery, he will find himself struggling to choose among the hundreds of bulky volumes, and wondering at the large number of men who have endured toil and hardship in distant lands in search of the new and strange. He might notice, too, how many of these stories have taken place since the 1800s. There were great discoveries of new lands in former times, but during the nineteenth and twentieth centuries, men have explored the earth's continents and islands, seeking their hidden secrets. Daring travelers have penetrated to the inmost recesses of distant lands, climbed the highest mountains, ventured among the most primitive tribes, soared into the highest regions of sky and space, studied a thousand regions before unknown, and learned more about the marvels of nature and the secrets of the earth than had been done in two thousand years before.

There was no part of the earth where these daring men did not go. They explored Africa and America, Asia and Australia; they went over the most dismal deserts and through the most distant islands; now under the scorching sun of the equator and now amid the freezing winds of the sea of ice, and a thousand books cannot begin to tell the story of what they saw and learned. Of course, I cannot tell you much about this long story, but I trust the time will come when you will read many of these books of travel and adventure for yourselves. In this chapter, I will help you take a rapid glance at what has been done in the frozen seas.

In the far north, you know, there is ice and snow all the year round, and travelers there have endured severe suffering and great pain. Ship after ship has gone there, some of them trying to find a channel for trading vessels around the tops of the continents, but finding only waters which the bitter cold had changed into ice as hard as rock. You have heard the names of some of these daring men. When you see on a map or in your travels the Hudson River in New York State and Hudson Bay in Canada, you may be reminded of the bold discoverer, Captain Henry Hudson, who, four hundred years ago, sailed up that river and into that bay. He was seeking a passage through the ice, and was not trying to find the North Pole, but he came within six hundred miles of it as long ago as 1607.

We cannot go far in this story without meeting tales of suffering and death. In 1845 Sir John Franklin, a bold British sea captain, sailed to the Arctic Ocean to try, like Hudson, to discover a northwest passage around America. He never came again from that dread sea of ice. On the 19th of May his two ships, the *Erebus* and *Terror*, were seen by a whaling vessel in Melville Bay, and that was the last that was ever seen of his ships and men. They vanished forever in the frozen wastes. Franklin and his bold followers became victims to the beast of the north.

Did no one try to find them? you ask. Yes, indeed; nobody was ever sought for more diligently. Ship after ship was sent out by Lady Franklin and others, until, during the next ten years, no less than fifteen expeditions left England and America in search of the lost navigator. Some few relics were found and the bones of some of the poor fellows; that was all, not a living soul of them was ever seen again. After that nobody wanted anything to do with the Northwest Passage. A passage blocked up with Arctic ice would have been as hard to traverse as to sail up the Falls of Niagara.

In 1881 another expedition went north that met with terrible disaster. This was commanded by Lieutenant Greely, of the United States army. His mission was to go as far north as he could and make a study of the weather and other conditions of the northern seas. Poor fellows! their ships were frozen in, and for three years they were left in a prison of ice. No relief came to them and nearly all their food was eaten. At last they had to leave their ships and make their way south through those terrible seas. They hoped to find food at Cape Sabine in Greenland, but not an ounce had been left for them, and there they had to stay through a dreadful Arctic winter, slowly starving to death. In June 1884, Commodore Schley came with a vessel to their relief. He found only six of them alive. The rest had died for want of food. These six were wasted almost to skeletons. A few days more and not one of all that gallant crew would have been alive.

That was dreadful enough, was it not? I should be glad if it was all, but there is another terrible story to tell. In 1879 a ship named the *Jeannette*, under Commander DeLong, went to the seas north of Siberia, in Russia, to try and push north in that frozen region. But the ice caught the strong ship and crushed it as if it had been an eggshell, and the captain and crew had to make their way southward in boats. They suffered dreadfully from cold and hunger. At length they came to the coast of Siberia at the mouth of the great Lena River. Here their food gave out, and they had starvation to fight as well as the bitter cold. Poor DeLong and all the men who came with him died in misery.

You may see from this that the sea of ice guards its secret well; the beast of the north lies in wait for those who venture within its reach. Many others have felt the pinch of its claws, but none have suffered as severely as those I have named. If I should try to tell the stories of all these bold explorers I could fill a book, so I must confine myself to one or two more. Of the men who set out to reach the Pole, one of the most successful was Dr. Fridtjof Nansen, a stalwart and daring son of Norway, who set out in 1893 on one of the most wonderful voyages ever made.

Nansen built himself a vessel called the *Fram*, which was as strong as solid wood and firm iron could make it, and of such a shape that the pressure of the ice would lift it up out of danger and carry it in a sort of ice cradle. He was not afraid of being frozen in. That was just what he wanted. He was convinced that there was a great current in the Arctic seas, and that if he got the *Fram* in a cradle of ice, it would be carried past the North Pole.

Away went the bold Nansen and vanished from sight. For three years he and his men were lost, and no one expected ever to see them again. People thought they had met the same fate as Sir John Franklin and his crew. Then, in 1896, the news flashed around the world that Nansen was home again and had been farther north than any man before.

The story he had to tell was wonderful. For nearly two years the *Fram* had drifted slowly to the north. But it went too slow to suit the impatient spirit of the daring Norwegian, and in March 1895, Nansen left the ship with one companion, and with dogs and sleds tried to make a rapid run over the frozen sea. He got to less than 300 miles from the Pole. But the ice was rough and broken, his dogs were weak and sick, and his food was getting low. If he hoped to see Europe again he had to turn back. He would have done as well to stay in the ship, for it drifted on till it was only about twenty miles south of where he stopped with his dogs, and then turned and made its way safely back to Europe.

Nansen and Johansen, his companion, got to the islands of Franz Joseph Land, off the furthest northern shore of Russia, where they spent a frightfully cold winter. But there were bears and walruses on the ice, and with the aid of their rifles they were able to hunt food to eat. In the spring they began walking southward and happily met Dr. Jackson, an English explorer, who had spent two years on those bleak islands. You may be sure that the gallant Nansen was glad enough to meet a fellow adventurer on that ice-bound shore. Together they all three made their way home. When Nansen arrived back in Europe he was greeted everywhere as a hero of the seas. He was one of the fortunate arctic explorers who came out of the frozen north alive.

Now there was another unfortunate explorer, who tried to reach the Pole in the way an eagle would go, through the air. After all, men had tried ships and men had tried sleds, and no one had succeeded. This adventurous man, a Swede named Andree, thought the best way to get to the Pole was by balloon. He knew a great deal about balloons, and he found that he could steer one away from the course of the wind by the use of a rubber sail and a drag-rope. So he had a strong balloon made, and in the summer of 1897 set out with two companions, with warm hopes of being back again within a few months, having finally reached the North Pole.

Poor fellow! something went wrong with his plans or with his balloon. The years passed by and no word came from Andree or his comrades. Searchers looked for them far and wide, but no trace of them was found.

But finally, an American lieutenant entered the beast-of-the-north's lair and conquered him. Robert E. Peary set out in 1891, determined to get to the Pole. He landed his ship far up on the Greenland coast, and then set out on snowshoes and with dog sleds across the northern edge of that great island. Only one man was with him, and they journeyed 650 miles across a plain of ice and snow to the far northeast coast. Here the ice ended, and there were broken stones over which he could not take his sleds. He was forced to turn back.

The brave Peary made another trial in 1896, with no better success, and in 1898 he set out again, bound to reach the Pole if it could be done. He was going to stay for years in the far north, planting depots of food far apart, and so going north step by step until he could set foot, if possible, on that mysterious Pole. He studied the methods that the Inuits used, the people that you may know as Eskimos. He learned to build igloos to survive the bitter winds. He dressed in furs and learned to hunt and preserve meat, and he hired Inuit men to be his helpers.

He kept trying. In 1902, in 1905, and in 1906, he kept pressing forward, trying now to go north from Canada instead of Greenland. Finally, in 1908, he set out on his final expedition. He set up a camp on Ellesmere Island, which you may find on a map if you look at a group of islands along the northern edge of Canada. Then, in March of 1909, Peary and five companions began the last stage of their journey. Using dogsleds and snowshoes, they trudged always northward, day after day, until finally, on April 7, Peary was able to make a jubilant entry in his journal: "The Pole at last!!! The prize of three centuries, my dream and ambition for 23 years. Mine at last."

The Pole had at last been reached. The beast of the north was conquered. Now the eyes of adventurous men would have to seek out a different goal: the highest mountain, the deepest sea, the dark reaches of space. But those stories must wait for chapters of their own.

Chapter 8

Waves Around the World

Sometimes, when a great invention appears on the world's stage, it is the work of one man who conceived of a great idea and labored over it until it bore fruit. But sometimes inventions that change the world are not the work of one but many, where each man studies the work of those who have gone before him and takes the next step. And sometimes, several people are working on the same idea at the same time, often without knowing anything about each other. This is what happened with radio.

I am certain that all of my readers have listened to a radio, perhaps at home to provide soft music during dinnertime, or in the car as your mother goes about her errands. Have you ever wondered how a radio works? It is a marvelous thing, but to understand it we must go deep down into the smallest particles that make up our world, and observe what they do.

If you were to wrap a wire around a piece of metal and run electricity through it, the metal would become magnetic, and it would put out a halo, or field, of electromagnetic waves: radio waves. These waves are streams of the tiniest particles that you can imagine, so small that they cannot be seen by even the most powerful microscope. The wonderful thing about these waves is that they can carry sound, so that the sound can be sent through the air and heard by someone many miles away. This is called "transmitting."

To transmit sound with a radio, you need two devices: a transmitter with a tall antenna to send out the waves carrying the sound, and a receiver, also with an antenna, to catch the waves as they strike it, extract the sound they are carrying, and reproduce the sound on a speaker so that you can listen to it. The radio in your car or your house is actually the receiver. The transmitter is the radio station somewhere in your town or city, a building bristling with tall antennae.

Who in the world could have created such a clever device? Well, it wasn't just one "who"; it was many.

Before radio could even be thought of, someone needed to discover the existence of the electromagnetic waves. People were thinking about that as far back as 1820, when a Danish chemist named Hans Christian Orsted ran electricity through a wire and noticed that it caused the needle on a compass to move. In 1831, a great scientist named Michael Faraday performed experiments that showed that the electromagnetic forces were moving out away from the wire, through the air itself. His work inspired another scientist, James Clerk Maxwell, to try to show, using mathematics, that the electromagnetic forces were moving in waves. Another man, Heinrich Hertz, proved that Maxwell was right by building a little machine to send out some electromagnetic radio waves and another little machine to detect them from a distance away. In 1866, an American dentist named Mahon Loomis stood on top of a mountain in the Blue Ridge country of Virginia and attached a transmitter to a kite and sent it aloft so that it would act as an antenna. He had sent another kite aloft fourteen miles away on the summit of a different mountain with an electrical meter attached, and, sure enough, the second kite received a signal from the first one.

All of these men, and others like them, were showing that the electromagnetic radio waves existed and were moving through the air, but no one had yet found a way to attach sound to them. Meanwhile, the telegraph and the telephone were invented, but they both used wires to transmit sound. Surely there must be a way to transmit the sound right through the air, carried by the radio wave! Many, many scientists and inventors were certain that there was, and throughout the 1800s, they all tried to find a way.

In 1891 a man named Nikola Tesla began to research radio waves. He was an electrical engineer from Serbia, in Austria, who had moved to the United States to work for Thomas Edison, and he was the sort of scientist who was interested in twenty different things at one time. But radio waves fascinated him; he was convinced that they could be of immense value to humankind if only a way could be found to control them. He believed that the waves could be transmitted right through the earth itself. In his laboratory, amongst all of his other electrical experiments, Tesla began building radio wave transmitters.

Meanwhile, in Italy, a young man named Guglielmo Marconi had been reading about the work of Heinrich Hertz. He began to conduct experiments, building most of his own equipment in the attic of his house in Italy, with the help of his butler, Mignani. First he built a storm alarm, with a bell that would ring whenever there was lightning. Then he built a device that would ring a bell on the other side of the room when he pushed a button beside his desk. By 1895 he had moved his experiments outdoors so that he could build taller and more powerful antennae. Soon he was able to transmit his signals over a hilltop to an antenna more than a mile away. His goal was to find a practical way to use the radio waves to carry sound, a way that would be affordable so that everyone could use it.

Back in the United States, Nikola Tesla had found better and better ways to control the radio waves. He built powerful antennae, and, in 1895, was preparing to transmit a radio signal 50 miles away. But then, disaster struck: a fire consumed his laboratory, destroying all of his work.

Marconi had moved his experiments to Great Britain; he was attempting to send a radio signal across the English Channel to

France. He built an antenna tower on both sides, and, on May 13, 1897, he transmitted a signal across the gray, choppy water.

This signal, though, like all of the others sent out by Tesla and other scientists, was not a sound. It was Morse code, where the electrical waves are sent out in interrupted bursts, short and long, that together can be translated into letters and words by whoever receives them.

Then, in 1900, Father Roberto Landell de Noura, a priest in the city of Sao Paulo, Brazil, invited the journalists in his city to attend a demonstration. He would, he told them, transmit a human voice through the air on a radio wave, without the aid of wires. The newspapermen were skeptical, but they came. They were ushered into a room to stand in front of a wireless receiver, and then nearly fell over themselves in amazement when a human voice began to address them. It was Father Landell, talking to them from another part of the city almost five miles away. Father Landell had found a way to "modulate" the radio waves: this means he had changed them so that they would carry the sound along with them as they radiated out from the transmitter.

Now that it was possible to transmit sound, the inventors began to scramble. Each wanted to be the man to build a workable system for the radio waves, so that they could be used by whole communities of people, even whole nations. Each wanted to claim that he was first, that he was the inventor of radio. Tesla began to build a huge tower in England, to be the first of a giant network of towers, transmitting all across the country. Marconi managed, in 1901, to transmit and receive signals across the Atlantic Ocean. He also had a plan to put transmitters and receivers in ships, so that they could communicate, for the first time in history, from the middle of the ocean. Father Landell left Brazil and came to America to try to forward his own claim of being first to transmit a voice and to find someone who would support his own research. All of these inventors looked upon each other with deep suspicion, and no one could know who was truly the inventor of radio.

At first the United States government declared that Marconi was the inventor. He received the patent, which means that only he could build the transmitters and receivers that the government would use. Father Landell tried to argue that he should have the patent, for he had been the first to transmit sound. But he was a foreigner with little support, and so his voice went unheard. Tesla claimed, perhaps rightly, that he had been first, even though the fire had destroyed his work.

Who was right? Who can say?

In 1943 the United States reversed its decision and awarded the patent for radio to Tesla, although by then, of course, it hardly mattered. Tesla was dead and gone by that point, and radio was alive and well, with towering antennae transmitting across the countryside and around the world.

Radio was the work of many men, and even now we cannot know who should be called the "Inventor of Radio." But we do know that it has been an important invention indeed. The electromagnetic radio waves fly through the air all around us, carrying music and voice to every home and car. Radio truly changed the world.

Chapter 9

The Prizes of Alfred Nobel

Alfred Nobel was born in Sweden in 1833. This birth of a third son must have lifted the spirits of Immanuel Nobel during what was a very difficult year. Immanuel Nobel was an engineer and builder, a man always interested in finding new and better ways to construct buildings and bridges. In 1833, though, he suffered the grave misfortune of losing several barges full of expensive building materials, and shortly after his little son was born, he was forced to close his business. Very little new work could he find, and eventually, in 1837, he left for Russia, hoping to start a new business there to support his family.

During the course of his construction work, Immanuel had learned a great deal about explosives, which an engineer uses to blast rock and other obstacles out of the way of the structure that he is building. In Russia, Immanuel began to experiment with using explosives as weapons for the Russian army. He opened a workshop that devoted itself to manufacturing mines, which are underwater bombs used for attacking ships. The Russian Tsar himself was pleased with Immanuel's work and commended him. Eventually, by the year 1842, Immanuel felt able to bring his family to Russia, and little Alfred was finally reunited with his father. A little more than one year later, Alfred's youngest brother Emil was born.

Alfred, a school-age boy by this time, was something of a

puzzle to his father. He was interested in his father's work, and in chemistry and other branches of science, but he was also passionately devoted to poetry and literature and the study of languages. By the time he reached the age of 17, Alfred could speak fluently not only his native Swedish, but also Russian, English, French, and German. Immanuel encouraged the study of science and mathematics and tolerated the language study, but he considered Alfred's interest in things like art and literature to be a waste of valuable time. When Alfred announced to his family his desire to be a writer, Immanuel decided that something drastic would have to be done. So he sent his son off to the United States, and then to Paris, to study chemistry.

While he was in Paris, Alfred met a young chemist from Italy, Ascanio Sobrero. Just a few years earlier, Sobrero had invented an entirely new form of explosive, a liquid called nitroglycerin. This liquid created huge explosions that could remove tons of rock with one blow. But it was dangerous; even the slightest bump could cause it to explode unexpectedly, and this made it difficult, and frightening, to use.

Alfred was fascinated with nitroglycerin. He saw at once how effective it could be, especially for miners and road builders. But before it could be used, a way must be found to control it.

Meanwhile, back in Russia, Immanuel's business affairs were booming. The Russians were involved in a war with their neighbors, and the Russian army was demanding more of Immanuel's weapons. Alfred went back to Russia to help in the family's business. With his father, he shared his hopes for nitroglycerin; if it could be made safer, what a boon to construction it would be! His father agreed, and he and Alfred began to experiment, trying to find a way to make the liquid more stable, so that it would explode only where and when someone wanted it to.

Their good fortune did not last. As soon as the Russians were no longer at war, they had no need of Immanuel's weapons. By 1863 Immanuel's business was forced to close. The two oldest

Nobel brothers, Robert and Ludvig, stayed in Russia to see if they could find any new business there for the family to pursue. Immanuel and the two younger brothers, Alfred and Emil, moved back to Sweden, to the city of Stockholm.

Now, more than ever, Alfred pinned his hopes on developing nitroglycerin into a safe explosive. It was not easy. Several times the nitroglycerin with which he or his father or brother were working exploded unexpectedly, demolishing a workbench or a storage room. And then, on September 3, 1864, a horrific blast ripped through the family's laboratory in downtown Stockholm. When the dust and smoke cleared, Alfred and his father discovered, to their horror, that the unstable nitroglycerin had killed the youngest Nobel brother, Emil.

The city leaders of Stockholm immediately banned any more experiments with explosives within the city limits. In his grief, Immanuel agreed and participated no more in the quest to tame nitroglycerin.

But Alfred, despite the terrible loss of his brother, remained convinced that the research must continue. He moved his experiments out of the city, onto a barge in the middle of a nearby lake.

Alfred knew by this time that the only way to make the deadly liquid safe was to mix it with something else. He began adding all sorts of different materials to it, trying to find a safe combination. Eventually, later in 1864, he found that by mixing the nitroglycerin with a certain type of clay, he could change it from a liquid into a paste. The paste he formed into rods, the most useful shape for construction because the explosive could then be fitted into holes drilled in rock. When the nitroglycerin was mixed with the clay, it was no longer unstable and prone to violent accidental explosion. In 1867 Alfred filed a patent on his nitroglycerin rods. Filing a patent meant that the invention needed a name. At first, Alfred considered calling the rods "Nobel's Safety Powder," which would provide the proper emphasis on the rods' stable and safe nature. But that name did not seem quite catchy enough, and eventually Alfred settled on a different name, from the Greek word for "power": dynamite.

Now Alfred must devise a way to make the dynamite rods explode only when and where they were needed. The dynamite could be ignited with just a tiny spark, so Alfred invented a way to deliver that spark to the rod just when it was needed: he fitted each rod with a "blasting cap," a tiny amount of very sensitive explosive powder. One end of the cap was attached to the dynamite and the other end was attached to a long fuse. When someone wanted to explode the dynamite, they needed only to light the fuse with a match and then move away, When the fuse burned down to the blasting cap, it would ignite the explosive powder, and the spark from the powder would then cause the whole dynamite rod to explode, right where it was needed.

Alfred continued to work with dynamite for the rest of his life, trying to make it more powerful and less dangerous. By the end of his life he had 355 different patents, most of them for different kinds of explosives.

All over the world engineers, bridge builders, road workers, and miners began using dynamite. It quickly became indispensable for all kinds of construction, and it made Alfred Nobel a very, very wealthy man.

In 1888 Alfred's older brother Ludwig died while on a trip to France. A French newspaper editor mistakenly thought that it was Alfred who had died and published an obituary, which is a summary of someone's life after they have died. The headline above the obituary cried in large letters, "The Merchant of Death is Dead!" It went on to say, "Dr. Alfred Nobel, who became rich by finding ways to kill more people faster than ever before, died yesterday."

Alfred was horrified when he read this. His purpose in creating dynamite had always been to assist engineers and construction workers, not to make bombs. Yes, others had taken his invention and used it in terrible ways, but that was not his intention.

Alfred began to feel very troubled in his mind about the way he would be remembered after his death. He was getting older, after all, and he must consider the future. For several more years, he brooded about this problem, and then he decided to take action. On November 27, 1895, he called in his lawyers and several witnesses, and signed before them his last will and testament, in which he had done a remarkable thing. The will set aside most of his enormous fortune to establish a set of prizes, to be awarded every year to people who had given "the greatest benefit to mankind."

Three of these prizes are for science, to be given to one scientist each in the fields of physical science, chemistry, and medicine. A fourth prize is given to a writer who produces a great book, and a fifth to a person or group of people who in some way further the cause of peace in the world.

Alfred died on December 10, 1896, comforted by the fact that, though his riches had been gained by an invention that some people considered evil, his wealth would forever after be used only for good. Alfred hoped that the prizes would inspire scientists and writers and peacemakers to continue their efforts for the benefit of all people.

The first of the Nobel Prizes were awarded in 1901, in Oslo, Norway. A group of Alfred's friends had organized the Nobel Foundation to take care of the money and give out the prizes each year. And except for the terrible years of World War II, when Norway was occupied by Germany, they have done just that. Every year, the winners of that year's prizes gather together in Stockholm, the capital city of Sweden. For several days, they give speeches to the large crowds that come from all across the world, and then, on December 10th, which is the anniversary of Alfred's death, each of the prize winners is presented with a gold medal by the king of Sweden and a large amount of money by the Nobel Foundation. Then they retire to Stockholm's City Hall and partake of an elegant banquet to which 1,300 people are invited.

Alfred wanted most of all to promote the good of mankind. Didn't he choose a most interesting way to do so?

Chapter 10

Marie Curie

On a cold November day in 1867, the Sklodowski family welcomed baby Marie, the fifth child to be born into their close-knit group. They were a Polish family, and very proud of it, too; but to be Polish was a difficult thing in those days. Poland did not even exist as its own independent nation; it had been divided up among other nations. The city of Warsaw, where the Sklodowski family lived, was controlled by Russia and its faraway tsar, who was determined to stamp out anything that remained of Poland. The people were forbidden to study Polish culture or learn the Polish language. Marie's family, though, were Polish patriots. Her parents, who were both teachers, did all that they could to secretly educate their students and their own children about their Polish heritage.

This was a dangerous course. The Russian authorities were suspicious of the family, and the Sklodowski's children and their students knew from a young age that they must be very careful. Marie wrote later, "Constantly held in suspicion and spied upon, the children knew that a single conversation in Polish, or an imprudent word, might seriously harm not only themselves, but also their families." Eventually, Marie's father was fired from his teaching position because of his Polish sympathies, and the family began to struggle for money to live on. And then, in 1878, Marie's mother died, plunging the whole family into deep and lasting sadness. Marie, who was ten years old that sad year, could not stop crying for weeks. But then she and her sisters invented a game, pretending that they were genius doctors who found miracle cures to heal the sick. Marie began to dream of using science and medicine for the good of all mankind.

Through all of this, Marie continued attending school and doing her best, even if it meant that she must do all of her lessons in the hated Russian language. She was the star pupil in her class, and when she graduated at age 15, she was awarded the school's gold medal. She hoped to go on with her schooling; her brother Josef had entered the medical school at the University of Warsaw, and she would have liked to do the same. But women were not allowed to study there, and so Marie and her sister Bronya were forced to find another way to study. They began to attend Warsaw's Floating University.

Are you imagining brick buildings floating up among the clouds? Actually, this school got its name from the fact that its classes met at night, changing its location every week to avoid the watchful eyes of the Russian authorities. The classes were taught by professors who, like Marie's parents, were educators and Polish patriots. Marie and Bronya studied at the Floating University for several years, but they both wanted desperately to leave Warsaw and travel to Paris, where they could study at a real university. But how could this be done? The family was poor; there was no money available to support two daughters studying in a foreign country.

Marie and Bronya made a pact: Marie would go out and find work, and she would pay for Bronya's tuition at a medical school in Paris. Then Bronya would work and pay for Marie to attend the university. Working together, they could both realize their dreams.

So, at age 17, Marie left Warsaw to become a governess for a family of seventeen children, the offspring of a scientist who ran a beet-sugar factory in a village far to the north of Warsaw. The teaching of the children was hardly enough work to fill her long days, and so she began to study. She read great works of literature and large science textbooks. She studied advanced mathematics. She took chemistry lessons from a chemist in the sugar factory. It became clear that she had a talent and love for science, especially physics, which is the science of light and gravity and all of the other forces that power our universe at its deepest level.

Marie worked hard, faithfully sending money to Bronya each month. By the fall of 1891, Bronya had finished her medical training, and it was Marie's turn to enter the University. She arrived in Paris in November, filled with happiness. She wrote about it later: "So it was in November 1891, at the age of 24, that I was able to realize the dream that had been constantly in my mind for several years."

Marie found an apartment in a small garret under the eaves, on the fourth floor of a large house. It was drafty and cold; the only furniture, a bed and one chair and a little stove with one burner to cook upon. In the winter months, Marie had to wear every piece of clothing she owned to keep warm. But her determination and excitement about what she was learning more than made up for her frugal living arrangements. She studied all day, every day, immersing herself in physics. Her diligence paid off when she graduated first in her class with her degree in physics in 1893, and second in her class with a degree in mathematics the next year. She also received a commission from a science society to do a study of the chemical makeup of steel.

To do this work she needed to find a laboratory, and she mentioned this need to a friend. The friend remembered that he had a colleague who might be able to help, a physicist named Pierre Curie. He was the chief of the laboratory at a Physics and Chemistry School in Paris. Would he be able to find room for Miss Sklodowski to work? Pierre thought that he would, and arranged to meet Marie, a meeting that would change the course of both their lives.

Marie liked Pierre. She wrote, "I noticed the grave and

gentle expression on his face, as well as a certain abandon in his attitude, suggesting the dreamer absorbed in his reflections." For his part, Pierre was smitten. Here was a young lady who loved science as much as he did, who could be a true partner for him both in his work and in his life. He wanted very much to marry her. Marie hesitated, though, because she felt that, by marrying a Frenchman, she would be abandoning her beloved Poland and her fiercely patriotic Polish family. But Pierre won her heart. Marie said later, "Our work drew us closer and closer, until we were both convinced that neither of us could find a better life companion." Pierre and Marie were married in July of 1895. For a honeymoon trip, they toured all over France on bicycles.

As she and Pierre settled their little household and welcomed the birth of daughter Irene in 1897, Marie was thinking about her career as a scientist. She wanted to become a doctor of science, which is the highest level of education that a scientist can attain. At that time in history, no woman had ever achieved a doctorate. Marie was determined to be the first.

In order to reach this goal, Marie needed to choose a topic to research: something that no other scientists in France were working on. Fortunately, an interesting subject presented itself to her at once. A French scientist named Henri Becquerel had just reported a discovery to the French Academy of Science: he had been studying uranium, a mineral that is found in the earth's crust, and he had found that the uranium was sending out some sort of mysterious, invisible ray. He had found it by accident when he had left some camera film near the uranium samples, and the film had become clouded, even though the uranium had never actually touched it. Marie read about this discovery, and it intrigued her. She decided that she would work with the uranium and try to discover the source of the energy that was radiating out from it, and then see if she could find that same energy in other minerals. She even made up a new word to describe the energy rays: "radioactivity."

Other physicists were guessing that the radioactive energy

must be coming from some interaction of the elements, the different ingredients, that made up uranium ore rocks. Marie had a strikingly different idea; she proposed that the radiation was coming from within the uranium atoms themselves. This was a bold idea. At that time, some scientists were not even entirely sure that atoms existed, and others were certain that the atom was the smallest possible thing. Certainly no one had given any thought to what might be *inside* an atom. But by measuring the radiation, Marie had noticed that it grew more intense in rocks with a larger portion of uranium in them, and this seemed to show that the uranium itself was radioactive.

Marie's research so interested Pierre that he gave up his own work, which was with crystals, and began to work alongside his wife. He and Marie spent several years working to isolate the radioactive part of the uranium ore. It was a difficult task, to break apart huge amounts of ore and separate out all of its different elements, looking for the tiny portion of the uranium that was radioactive. They had to work over a large vat in an abandoned shed in the school courtyard, with drafty walls and a leaky roof. By 1898, Marie had discovered an entirely new element which she and Pierre named Radium, after "radiation." By 1902, after purifying and breaking apart one ton of rock, Marie and Pierre had isolated a tiny amount of pure radium.

In 1903 Marie and Pierre were awarded the Nobel Prize in Physics for their work with radiation. But they were neither of them able to travel to Sweden to receive their prize. They were both sick.

You see, radium is dangerous, although neither Pierre nor Marie knew it. They were both captivated by its beauty. The radium gave off a soft blue light that glowed in the dark, so lovely that Marie kept a clear glass tube filled with radium beside her bed, and often carried glowing tubes of radioactive liquid in her skirt pocket. She remarked that "one of our joys was to go into our workroom at night. The glowing tubes looked like faint, fairy lights." But the radiation that produced the glow was also harming Marie and Pierre's bodies every day as they worked with it. Their fingertips were scarred and burned, their legs and arms ached; they both felt constantly tired, as if they could barely move. Pierre become so sick he could no longer work; Marie kept on, though she was thin and exhausted.

Then, in 1906, Pierre was struck by a horse-drawn carriage in a Paris street and killed.

Marie was heartbroken; she wrote that she had suddenly become "an incurably and wretchedly lonely person." But she kept working. She was certain that radium would be of great benefit to all mankind, and she continued to strive for that goal, working in her laboratory every single day. Her efforts did not go unnoticed, for, in 1911, she received a second Nobel prize, this time for Chemistry. She accepted the prize and kept on working. She found a way to use radium in portable x-ray machines, so that doctors could easily see inside a human body. During World War I, a huge conflict about which you will soon read, she and her daughter labored tirelessly on the battle lines in France, using their x-ray machines, which were called *petit curies*, to help wounded soldiers.

After the war, Marie and other scientists discovered that radium could be used to fight diseases like cancer, because the radiation would kill the deadly cancer cells inside of a sick person.

Marie died in 1934, a victim of the dangerous radiation to which she had dedicated most of her life. She was the first woman to win a Nobel Prize, and the first person to win two. She is one of only two scientists who have won the Prize in two different kinds of science. The work that she and Pierre did opened the mysterious world of the atom to many other scientists, and the atom and its secrets are still being explored today.

Chapter 11

On a Beam of Light

Have you ever wondered what it would be like to ride upon a beam of light? In the first years of the twentieth century, there lived a young man who wondered about that. In fact, he wondered about a lot of things, and what became of his wondering you shall see.

In 1905 Albert Einstein spent his days in an office in the Swiss city of Bern, working as a patent clerk. He helped inventors fill out the paperwork so they would own their creations and no one else could claim them. He typed out the forms and filed them in their proper places, chatted with his friend in the office next door, and ate his simple lunch every day at his desk. When evening softened the sky, he walked home and greeted his wife and newborn son, and then shared with them a dinner of beef and potatoes, or pea soup and cabbage.

But all the while he was doing these normal, homely deeds, his mind was somewhere else. He might be typing or chatting or eating, but he was thinking about light and time. Every surface in his little study was buried under stacks of paper, and each paper was covered with lines of handwritten notes and mathematical symbols, as he tried to fathom the answer to his question: what *would* it be like to ride upon a beam of light?

Einstein had read the works of the scientists who had gone before him, and he was humble before their great thinking. But he had realized in the last few years that all of modern science, and all of ancient science too, had barely scratched the surface of the magnificence that was reality. The universe and our world within it seemed to him to be a puzzle of the most magnificent proportions, and the scientists thus far had truly fit together only a piece or two.

One of the men whose work he was following was a German physicist named Max Planck. Remember, a physicist is someone who studies the nature of our universe itself: light, gravity, time, and space. Planck had discovered that light delivered itself in little packets. In other words, light is not a single big thing, but is instead a lot of very tiny things. Einstein was fascinated by this idea. He had also read the work of a Scottish scientist named James Clerk Maxwell, who said that light must travel in a wave, and now Einstein put those two ideas together. What if light traveled in a stream of individual particles? Einstein wrote it all up in a paper that was published by a science journal, a kind of magazine for scientists that contains all the latest thinking on scientific topics.

Then it was like a flood had been unleashed; Einstein began to write like mad. During the rest of that year he published three more papers, and each one contained ideas that no one had ever proposed before. The second paper that year discussed Einstein's ideas about atoms and molecules, the same subject that so interested Marie Curie. I'm certain that some of my readers may have learned already about these tiny particles, of which everything around us is composed; a raindrop, a sunflower, the skin of your hand—everything is made up of atoms, atoms combined together into little groups called molecules. Scientists in Einstein's day had long suspected that this must be true, and the work that Pierre and Marie Curie were doing with radioactivity seemed to show that atoms truly existed, but no one had ever actually seen an atom, because in those days there were still no microscopes powerful enough to see anything so small. Einstein wanted to prove that atoms and molecules were real. He put a tiny grain of pollen in a glass of water, knowing that it would start to move about, even if the water appeared absolutely still. Other scientists had noticed this phenomenon before; in fact, it already had a name: Brownian Motion, after a Scottish botanist who had described it in a paper in 1827. Einstein believed that the movement was caused by the motion of water molecules bumping against the pollen, and he showed, with his mathematical symbols, the zigzag path the molecules would take inside that glass of water. His paper proved that Brownian Motion is caused by the movement of atoms, and thus that atoms actually existed.

Suddenly, the name of "Einstein" began to be spoken in many scientific laboratories and classrooms around Europe. And then Einstein published his next two papers.

I want you to think carefully with me now, for it is difficult indeed for one humble author to explain to you in a paragraph or two the deep thoughts that are contained in these two papers. But these thoughts are important because they have made possible so much of our modern world, so I will do my best, and you will think it through with me.

Here is what Einstein said: Everyone knows from experience that speed is "relative"; that is, it changes depending on your position and motion. Think of it like this: suppose you were sitting on the very back bench of a bus, and you wanted to toss a ball up to your friend who is sitting on the first bench at the front. The bus is traveling down the street at 30 miles per hour, and you throw your ball to your friend at 10 miles per hour. To you and your friend, the ball appears to be going 10 miles per hour, and your friend easily catches it. But now suppose your sister is standing outside on the curb, watching the bus go by. She sees you toss the ball, but to her the ball looks as if it is whizzing by at 40 miles per hour, because she is seeing the motion of both the bus and the ball. Later, she might ask you, "Why did you throw the ball so hard at your friend?" You have experienced this yourself; think about when you are in a car speeding down the highway, and another car passes you. To you, that car looks to be going quite slowly, but to someone standing on the side of the road, that car is zooming.

But Einstein, in his paper, proposed that one speed is *not* relative: the speed of light. You might know that light travels very fast indeed: 186,000 miles every second. Einstein said that light stays at that speed no matter what, even if it is being observed by two people at the same time who are each traveling at totally different speeds. It does not matter if I am flying to Florida on a jet streaking through the sky at 1,000 miles per hour, and you are strolling on a beach at 2 miles per hour; the speed of light would be for either of us exactly the same.

What? I imagine you're saying. How can that possibly be true?

In order to explain this, Einstein knew that if the speed of light is always constant, something else must change. He proposed in his paper that the thing that changes is time. He said that, if you were able somehow to ride upon a beam of light, so that you were going almost as fast as the light itself, time would go more slowly for you. The faster you move, the slower time goes by.

This might seem impossible, but experiments have proven that Einstein was right. Scientists put a very precise clock on board an extremely fast jet and kept an identical clock upon the ground. After the jet had flown around the world as fast as it could, they compared the two clocks and found that the clock aboard the jet had ticked more slowly than the one that had stayed put.

Of course, we here on earth do not notice any of this. We are moving too slowly, and time remains the same for us.

Isn't that amazing thinking? And Einstein did this without a laboratory or a computer. All he had was pencils and paper, and his imagination. And he was not done thinking, not at all. He had many other ideas sparking through his mind.

As soon as this paper was published, scientists began to buzz about it. They called it Einstein's Theory of Relativity. Einstein did not join in the discussions; he continued his quiet work at the patent office, and he continued to think and write. He began to wonder about other things in addition to light and time. He wrote to his son, "I was sitting in the patent office in Bern when all of a sudden a thought occurred to me: if a person falls freely he won't feel his own weight. I was startled!" He turned all of his thoughts toward gravity, and he continued to produce papers so interesting and thought-provoking that finally, universities and colleges from all over the world began to write and offer him teaching positions. He ended up accepting such a position at the University of Berlin, and there he stayed for the next 18 years.

Einstein was concerned with gravity because his original theory of relativity did not take gravity into account, though of course gravity affects everything that moves in the universe. You, yourself, have seen gravity's effects whenever you drop a ball or fall down while playing tag! So Einstein wanted very much to write a new, expanded theory of relativity that would include gravity as well. He tried to answer some very basic questions: what is gravity? how does it work?

These are not easy questions. In one of his letters, Einstein wrote that "every step" of solving this problem "is devilishly difficult." But finally, in 1915, he was able to write joyously to his son that "I have just completed the most splendid work of my life!"

Here is what Einstein declared in his new General Theory of Relativity: space and time are really just one thing, and gravity happens when space and time are bent. Think of it like this: imagine a big rubber trampoline with a heavy bowling ball in the middle. The bowling ball would make the trampoline bend, would it not? And if you tried to roll a marble across the trampoline, what would happen? The marble would curve around and begin to circle the bowling ball. Well, Einstein said, the universe works like that. Space and time are the big trampoline, the sun is the heavy bowling ball, and the planets are the marbles that are rolling around the well that the sun makes in space. That "well" is gravity.

If I am right, Einstein said, the gravity around the sun would actually cause light itself to bend. And this proved true. In 1919 there was a solar eclipse, where the moon blocked the light of the sun for a short while on earth. Scientists in England measured the light from stars beyond the sun and discovered that Einstein was correct. Their light was indeed bent by the well of gravity around the sun.

After this, Einstein's fame knew no bounds. Everywhere he traveled, people clamored to hear him speak. He was the most beloved scientist in the world.

He accepted a new position at a university in Princeton, New Jersey, where he stayed until the end of his life. He worked very hard to use his fame for good causes. He spent five hours a day answering all the letters that people wrote to him, even letters from little children. And he continued to think. Until he died at age 76, he worked and wrote every day.

Why is Einstein so important? you might be thinking. His thoughts are interesting and amazing, but why do they matter?

The theories of Albert Einstein provide the foundation for many things that you and I use every day. The computer that this author used to write these words, the television set you might watch sometimes, the scanners that the clerks in the supermarket use when your mother buys groceries, the cell phone your father might use for his work: all of these things are based on the ideas that Einstein first proposed. Our modern world would be a very different place indeed if Albert Einstein had not wondered what it would be like to ride a beam of light.

Chapter 12

The War to End All Wars

As you have been reading about and studying the history of our world, you have probably noticed that history has always been marked by warfare, where two countries or peoples battle each other in order to gain territory, or right a wrong, or revenge a previous attack. What would you think, then, of a conflict called "The Great War" and "The War to End All Wars"? It sounds frightening, doesn't it: a war so large that it can have a name like that? But such a war did occur, between the years of 1914 and 1918. All the world's great powers came to be involved in it, and it was the largest war in history. Now, in our time, we look back and call it World War I.

The trigger that ignited this giant war was the death of a duke, an Austrian nobleman named Archduke Franz Ferdinand. I hope you remember learning a little bit about Austria in an earlier chapter of this book. By this point in history, Austria had joined with another nation, Hungary, to form an empire, and Franz Ferdinand was the crown prince, and the nephew of the emperor, Franz Josef. In June of 1914, Franz Ferdinand and his wife, the duchess Sophie, were sent by the emperor to the city of Sarajevo, which was the capital of a province called Bosnia. Many of the citizens of Bosnia were not particularly happy to have him come; the Bosnians wished fervently to be their own country rather than subservient to Austria, and they were supported in this by their neighbors, the Kingdom of Serbia.

Franz Ferdinand and Sophie arrived at the train station in Sarajevo on the morning of June 28 and climbed into a shining black open motorcar. But their driver made a mistake: he turned wrongly into a narrow, dead-end alley and, so, was obliged to put the car into reverse and slowly back out. Across the street, a young Serbian assassin named Gavrilo Princip could hardly believe his eyes. He had come prepared to shoot, but he had not expected his target to appear directly in front of him. Stepping quickly forward, he raised his gun and killed the Archduke.

News of this death was greeted in Austria with horror, but also with secret relief. The Austrians had been looking for any excuse to attack and conquer the troublesome Serbians, thus expanding their empire. They made plans to invade Serbia, but first they wished to secure the backing and support of Prussia, or Germany as it was increasingly coming to be called, with whom the Austrians had a treaty. And this gave the worried Serbians time to approach and beg support from the huge nation of Russia, with whom they also had a treaty.

And now I find I should explain what is meant by "having a treaty." A treaty is a formal agreement between two or more nations in which they agree to do something: stop fighting a war, trade favorably with each other, recognize a border between their two lands, or, most importantly for our story here, protect each other if attacked. So if Austria-Hungary invaded Serbia, Russia must step in to help fight Serbia's battle.

But there were more treaties than just those two involved. Russia also had treaties with France and Britain. Any Russian wars became French and British wars as well. So you can see that, when Austria-Hungary officially declared war on Serbia in July of 1914, many other European countries were already enmeshed in the conflict. In just a few weeks, Austria-Hungary and Germany were at war with Russia and France.

The nation of Germany had watched the dispute between Austria and Serbia with great interest, since the Germans had long wished to expand their own empire, and this seemed to provide an opportunity. But it was not an opportunity that came without risk. If you look on a map of Europe, you will see that Germany is situated between France and Russia, and so it would have to fight this war along two battle lines, or fronts, as they are called: a Western Front, facing France, and an Eastern Front along the border with Russia. The German war leaders had long considered the danger that fighting on two fronts represented, and they had come up with a plan years before to solve this very problem. It was called the Schleiffen Plan, and it looked like this: The Germans knew that it would take the Russians at least six weeks to muster an army and march toward Germany. During that six-week time, then, the Germans planned to invade the nation of Belgium, a small country that nestled along the English Channel directly between France and Germany. After taking control of Belgium, the Germans would march straight into France. They assumed that, if they struck hard and quick, the French would fall before them within six weeks, and they could then turn their attention back to Russia and its huge army. //

In August of 1914, the Germans put this plan into action.

The chain of treaties continued to pull more and more nations into the war, for the invaded country of Belgium had a longstanding treaty with Great Britain, and now Great Britain declared war on Germany in support of Belgium and France.

The German army marched steadily south toward Paris, and French and British troops, along with all their allies, moved northward to stop them. By September of 1914, the two immense forces had met and clashed in Belgium and eastern France, and neither side could force the other to back down. Unable to move forward and unwilling to move back, both armies began to dig trenches.

The soldiers dug deep ditches in the heavy clay soil, so that they could fire their guns at the enemy while remaining somewhat protected themselves. Soon there were trenches not only all along the front lines of the battle, but ranging backward for long distances, so that supplies and fresh soldiers could be brought to the Front with less risk. All in all, by the end of the war, the Western Front contained almost six thousand miles of trenches.

Life in the trenches was miserable for the poor men in both armies. The ditches were continually damp, sometimes filled knee-high with freezing water. The soldiers were always covered with mud and blue with cold, and they could not lift their heads above the level of the trench, for fear of being struck by an enemy's bullet. They fought by firing cannon, or artillery, at the other trench. But sometimes the officers would order the men to attack, and then they would have to brave the awful open space between themselves and the enemy's trench—a flat, mud-churned area covered with barbed wire, usually only fifty or sixty yards wide, which was called No Man's Land. So many soldiers lost their lives in No Man's Land that it became clear that eventually the side with the most men would prevail.

As the war dragged on, all through 1915 and 1916 and 1917, the trenches did not move. The war had become a stalemate; neither side was winning. And by 1917, Britain and France were running out of men.

Meanwhile, the Germans were also having to send men to fight the Russians on the Eastern Front. The Russians had used the war as an opportunity to advance as far into Germany as they could. By 1917, however, Russia was engulfed in the Russian Revolution, about which you will learn more soon, and was no longer interested in fighting any wars except the one it was engaged in with itself. When the Russian tsar, Nicholas II, was removed from power, the new government of Russia ended its participation in the war by signing a peace treaty with Germany on March 3, 1918.

Now Germany could focus all of its attention on the Western Front, and just in time, too, for a huge new threat had arisen. The Germans had made the mistake of provoking the United States.

The Americans had not wanted to join the war. To them, it seemed a European conflict—tragic, to be sure, but too far away to have any real effect. But the Germans changed that way of thinking. First, they began to sink ships with submarines, all kinds of ships, and some of those ships carried American passengers. Second, they sent a secret telegram to Mexico, a message that I am certain they wished they had not sent when all was over.

The telegram was sent in early 1917 by a German foreign minister, Arthur Zimmerman. In it, Zimmerman offered the leaders of Mexico a proposal of alliance. Join with us, it said, and if it becomes necessary for us to attack the United States, you will then be able to reconquer your lost territory in Texas, New Mexico, and Arizona.

Zimmermann and the Germans did not know, however, that the British had broken their secret codes and could read all of their telegrams. (That in itself is an exciting story that I hope you may read about some day.) At once, Great Britain sent their own message to the United States, including all of the contents of the German telegram. When the American people learned of Germany's offer to Mexico, their feelings about the war changed. No longer did it seem a far-off, impersonal conflict. Now it was real and very dangerous. In April of 1917, the United States declared war on Germany.

It was not a moment too soon. The French and British armies were exhausted and disheartened. Germany was moving all of its soldiers off the Eastern Front to the West. To the Western allies, Germany seemed unstoppable, and they looked to the Americans, with their seemingly limitless supplies of men and machinery, for salvation.

For one year more, the war lingered on, but the fresh supplies of men and enthusiasm that America contributed to the Western front made all the difference. For unbeknownst to the Allies, the Germans were running short: they had no more men, no more artillery, no more ability to make war. And finally, on the 11th hour of November 11, 1918, the war was officially ended.

All of the nations involved signed a peace treaty called the Treaty of Versailles. The War to End All Wars was over. But did it live up to its name? Did its horrors convince the nations of the world to shun all warfare and live in peace? I'm sorry to tell you that it did not, as you will see.

Chapter 13

The Christmas Truce

In December of 1914, as the Great War tightened its grip on Europe, soldiers from Britain and France crouched in long trenches dug deep into the soil of Belgium. Just a short distance away, Prussians and Saxons and Bavarians, the soldiers of Germany, huddled in their own cold trenches. Between the enemy lines ran a thin strip of muddy, trampled ground, the No Man's Land that each army needed to capture and yet had failed to do so. The soldiers and their leaders were trapped in the trenches, and neither army could make any progress forward. For miles and miles along the Western Front, the armies faced one another, allied in equal misery.

Winter rains made any movement a difficult, almost impossible, endeavor. The Belgian countryside consisted of miles of deep clay soil that quickly turned into a mass of sticky mud after only an hour or two of rain. The bitter winds were blown off the frigid North Sea, chilling a soldier to his bones. In the trenches, the men stayed where they were, and with only fifty or sixty yards of earth separating them from the opposing army, the soldiers began to know quite a lot about their enemies. They quickly learned all the routines of the soldiers on the other side: when they ate and slept, what games they liked to play, when they were more eager to fire their guns, and when they preferred to merely hunker down and endure the cold rain. Soon the familiarity led to something almost like friendship. From one side to the other, the soldiers began to exchange shouted comments, and sometimes throw tins of food back and forth, or newspapers weighted with a stone.

The commanders on both sides of No Man's Land knew that this could not continue. An army cannot fight a war when it has befriended its enemy! The British general issued a stern command to his troops: "Friendly intercourse with the enemy, however tempting and amusing it may sometimes be, is absolutely prohibited!"

But Christmas was fast approaching, and on both sides, the young soldiers were making such holiday preparations as they could. The Germans decorated the trenches with bits of paper and greenery, no easy feat with the acres of mud all around them. In the British trenches, each man received a package in the name of the King George V's daughter, Princess Mary, with a card from the King wishing them God's protection, a tin of sweets, and a plum pudding.

The Christmas spirit seemed to infect the soldiers, despite the miserable life they were leading in the trenches. One week before the holiday, some German troops smuggled a splendid chocolate cake to the British soldiers across from them, accompanied by a note written in painstaking English: "We propose a concert tonight, and we cordially invite you to attend—provided you will give us your word of honour as guests that you agree to cease all hostilities between 7:30 and 8:30. When you see us light candles at the edge of our trench, you can safely put your heads above your trenches, and we shall do the same, and begin the concert."

The British accepted the invitation. At 7:30 precisely that evening, eight German soldiers appeared atop their trench and began to sing. The British applauded wildly after each song, and finally the Germans invited them to sing along. After one hour the lights went out, and the little concert ended with some of the British men shooting their guns high into the clouds overhead.

All along the miles of the Front, the desire to celebrate

Christmas overcame the demands of war. The Germans began setting up Christmas trees along the tops of their trenches and decorating them with candles. On the night of December 23rd, thousands of glittering trees glowed in the darkness. Many curious British soldiers crawled out of the trenches into No Man's Land to investigate and came back to tell their officers that the Germans were determined to celebrate the holiday. Slowly and carefully, British leaders crept out into the darkness to meet with the German officers and many informal agreements were reached. Tomorrow, on Christmas Eve, there would be no gunfire. Unbeknownst to their leaders, the soldiers had declared a truce.

Have any of my readers ever experienced a truce? I am certain you have, even if you were not aware of the proper term. Can you recall the last time you were outside on a summer evening, playing tag with your friends? Suppose that, in the midst of your game, you heard your mother calling you. "Times!" you would shout, or "Time out!", and all of your friends would stop the game while you ran to answer your mother's summons. During the time-out, you could not be tagged; the game had been temporarily suspended. Well, a truce is like a time-out during a war. The battle is stopped for a certain amount of time; no guns are fired, no soldiers fight. If the truce becomes permanent, it is called an armistice.

I am certain that you can imagine the relief that a soldier feels when he knows that he is under the protection of a truce and will not have to fight that day.

What happened on that Christmas Eve in 1914 was not an official truce, but nevertheless it began to spread all the way along the Western Front. As the Germans in Belgium lighted the candles on their Christmas trees, they began to sing some of their favorite Christmas carols. One of the British soldiers described it in a letter home; "It was a beautiful moonlit night, frost on the ground, white almost everywhere; and there was a lot of commotion in the German trenches. And then they sang 'Silent Night'—'Stille Nacht.' I shall never forget it. It was one of the highlights of my life." When the Germans paused in their singing, the British soldiers responded with applause and carols of their own.

The German soldiers farther along the line began to put up hastily-written signboards that said, "YOU NO FIGHT, WE NO FIGHT" and "HAPPY CHRISTMAS." Cautiously, when they saw the British or French soldiers reading their signs, the German men would come out of their trenches, their hands spread wide to show that they carried no weapons. Soon the men were shouting Christmas greetings across No Man's Land, along with some good-natured teasing. "English soldiers!" the Germans shouted, "Where are your Christmas trees?"

The next morning, as Christmas Day dawned, the truce remained in place. But before the holiday could truly be celebrated, the soldiers all along the Front slipped out into No Man's Land in groups of twos and threes to perform a sad duty. There on the ground lay the bodies of many of their comrades who had fallen in the days before the truce. There had been no way to retrieve them and bury them until this quiet morning. Burial parties, German and British and French, completed their work in the early hours, secure in the knowledge that there would be no gunfire on this day. In many places, Germans and Britons worked together and held joint services to pray and honor their dead.

Farther down the line, in France, a British soldier named Henry Williamson wrote a story about that day, using the name Phillip Maddison. He described his shock when he looked out into No Man's Land on Christmas morning and found it filled with German and British soldiers, milling about and attempting to talk to one another despite not knowing the other's language. Maddison saw one of the Germans carefully writing his name and address down on a scrap of paper and giving it to a British soldier so that they could correspond after the war. One friendly German came up to Maddison and greeted him. "We watched you last night, putting up a wire fence there, but we wouldn't fire, even if we was ordered to." Maddison told him they had watched the

Germans putting up their Christmas trees the night before, and they hadn't fired either. The two young men exchanged buttons from their coats as souvenirs, and then Maddison continued up the line of trenches, looking about in amazement at all the friendly conversations. Then he stopped short. Up ahead, he saw a ball flying through the air, and several men chasing after it. *My goodness!* he thought. *They are playing football!*

Football, the game that my readers in the United States will know as soccer, was a favorite sport in England. And here were some men playing a match right in the middle of No Man's Land! Maddison lost no time in joining in.

In fact, football matches sprang up all along the Western Front that day, some behind the trenches and some in the middle, between German and British troops. Sometimes the Germans merely watched, being unfamiliar with the game. One young English officer wrote home that "It's really the most extraordinary state of affairs! We had an inter-platoon game of football in the afternoon; a cap stuffed with straw did for the ball, much to the Saxons' amusement." Another British soldier wrote, "Our men played football at the back of the trench, and the Germans walked about on top of their trench and watched. It was hard to think that we were at war with one another."

Philip Maddison, having finished the football match, had almost forgotten that fact as well. He was moving back along the trenches, trying to find his way back to his platoon. He knew that he was in the Germans' territory, but he was not terribly worried about it until he suddenly found himself face to face with a formidable German officer.

"May I have a word with you?" he asked Maddison, who swallowed and nodded, and quickly explained about the football game.

"I see." The officer looked at Maddison sternly. "May I count on your word that you will regard your recent visit behind our lines as not that of an agent?"

"An agent, sir?"

"A spy."

"Oh, no. I wasn't for a moment spying, sir." Maddison tried to keep his voice calm.

"I am glad to hear it," said the German, "for otherwise you would be my prisoner. Do you understand? We are still at war."

They were, indeed. The truce could not last. It was born in the hearts of common soldiers and not in the powerful commanders who directed the war. As Christmas Day faded into evening, slowly, all along the Western Front, the guns began to fire once more. The Christmas trees disappeared from the tops of the German trenches, and the British soldiers put away their footballs. No more voices were raised in song. The war would continue on for four more years. The truce was over.

Chapter 14

The Red Baron

D o you ever wonder how a man becomes a hero? Did you know that someone can be a hero even to his enemies? Now I will tell you the story of the Red Baron, Manfred von Richthofen, and you must decide if you would have thought him a hero if you had lived in the days of the Great War.

Long ago, during the last years of the nineteenth century, a boy roamed through the forests of Poland, hunting and fishing with his two brothers. These boys, Manfred, Lothar, and Bolko, had been born into a noble family, but they much preferred the delights of the outdoors to the luxuries of the castle that was their home. They stalked wild boar and elk through the trees and hunted pheasant and grouse with their sleek dogs. Manfred, especially, also loved riding horses and doing gymnastics.

At the time of this story, the land that we know of nowadays as Poland was actually part of the German empire, and so Manfred and his family thought of themselves as German. When he was eleven years old, Manfred was sent away to a military academy, just like most boys from noble families in Germany. There he learned math and languages and other school subjects, and also the disciplines and skills of a soldier. When he completed the academy in 1911, he joined a cavalry unit, which means a group of soldiers trained to fight on horseback.

And so, when the Great War began, Manfred was already a

part of the German army, and he and his unit were sent immediately to the Eastern Front to face the Russians. Soon it became very clear, though, that this War to End All Wars was impossible to fight on horseback. The new and terrible guns and the miles of barbed wire prevented the horsemen from fighting as they had been trained. Manfred's unit was sent back from the front line, assigned instead to the Quartermaster Corps. Every army has a quartermaster: his job is to make certain that food and supplies flow forward to the front lines and back again. Manfred was not a bit satisfied with this sort of work. He wrote to the commander asking for a transfer to a flying unit. "My dear Excellency," his letter said, "I have not gone to war to collect cheese and eggs." In May of 1915, his request was approved, even though he had not really expected that it would be. He was elated.

Manfred joined the German Army Air Service on the Western Front. At first he served as an observer, sitting behind the pilot of a fighter plane and watching the ground for enemy movements. But that was still not enough for Manfred, who had been such a hunter as a boy. He wanted to be the one behind the controls. So in October of 1915, he began training to be a pilot.

His first flight was not a success; he crashed his airplane while attempting to land! But as he continued to learn and practice, he quickly became an excellent flyer and was sent back to the Russian front to fly bombers.

Then in August of 1916, he encountered a legendary German pilot, Oswald Boelcke. Boelcke was an ace, a title given to any pilot who had prevailed over more than five enemy airplanes. Boelcke had downed more than forty. He was revered throughout Germany, and the army commanders had given him the task of recruiting young flyers for a new flying unit. After talking with Manfred, Boelcke told him to pack his bags; he would be returning to the Western Front to fly fighter planes.

In the German Air Service, a group of pilots along with their airplanes was known as a *jasta*, so Boelcke's new wing of fighters was called Jasta 2. They began flying over the battlefields of France in September 1916 and were immediately successful, shooting down several British fighter planes each day. On September 17th, Manfred managed to get behind a British plane with his fighter, coming so close, he said later, that he was afraid he might dash himself right into the Englishman. He brought the plane down with his machine gun and then landed his own plane to see what had become of the pilot. He had been killed. As he always would be, Manfred was respectful of his antagonists. He wrote, "I honored the fallen enemy by placing a stone on his beautiful grave."

After this, his first true victory in the air, Manfred sent an order to a silversmith in Berlin, asking for a tiny silver cup to be made, just two inches tall, and engraved with the date and the type of airplane that he had shot down.

Jasta 2 continued their daily battles, but then, in November, the men suffered a great loss. Their leader, Oswald Boelcke, was killed in a mid-air crash with another German airplane. Manfred saw it happen from the ground. In the funeral procession, he carried the revered ace's medals on a pillow.

By this time, Manfred had sent nine more orders off to the silversmith. Having ten "kills" marked Manfred as an ace in his own right, and his success only continued. On November 23rd of 1916, he shot down Britain's most decorated ace, Major Lanoe George Hawker, after a pitched battle that began high in the sky and ended just above the treetops. When he saw Hawker's plane fall, Manfred was elated but also somber. "He was a brave man, a sportsman, and a fighter," he said later of Hawker. Those were the highest words of praise that Manfred could give. Hawker was his eleventh victory.

After his 16th victory, Manfred was named leader of his own squadron, Jasta 11, and, as such, he enforced a certain set of rules both for the other pilots and for himself: Do not fly too low. Do not follow too closely. Do not get so involved in a battle that you lose track of where you are and fly too deeply into enemy territory. Manfred was not a risk-taker, and he expected his men to be careful and methodical in their daily skirmishes in the sky.

However, despite his careful ways, when he became squadron leader, Manfred decided to do something extraordinary: he painted his fighter plane, every part of it, bright red. Very soon, his men followed suit, painting parts of their planes red as a show of respect for their leader. Soon other Jasta units began to do the same, choosing a squadron color and painting their planes. In April of 1917, when Manfred was given command of a larger group of planes, composed of four Jastas, the colorful machines were so distinctive that the whole group became known as "the Flying Circus."

Manfred in his red plane was by far the most renowned. The German newspapers, eager for any sort of good news, showered him with adoration, and even the common soldiers down in the muddy trenches knew his exploits. He had acquired his own nickname, "the Red Baron," and all the British flying aces knew him and were determined to bring him down. By the end of June 1917, Manfred's collection of tiny silver cups numbered fifty-six.

Then, in July 1917, the unthinkable happened. The Red Baron was shot down! Two British fighter pilots, Commander A. E. Woodbridge and Captain D. C. Cunnell, encountered Manfred's plane high above the German front line and knew at once who it was. The two British fighters flew straight at Manfred, head on, firing their guns all the while. To their amazement, they saw the red plane point her nose suddenly downward, spinning round and round and then crashing heavily to the ground. *We've got him*, Cunnell thought jubilantly.

Indeed, they had wounded Manfred badly. Because his plane had gone done in German territory, he was rushed to the hospital at once. But despite the best treatment that the doctors could give, the wound never really healed properly and Manfred felt it for the rest of his life.

For a month he lay impatiently in the hospital, anxious to be flying again. When he did finally return to the air, he seemed to be different somehow. He went two full weeks before downing another plane, and he seemed less careful. Nevertheless, by September 1917 he had reached his 60th victory, more than any other pilot, German or British. There were no more little silver cups after this; silver had become too scarce in Germany, and Manfred did not want to accept any trophies made of a cheaper metal. When he downed his 64th fighter, he sent the pilot, who ended up in the hospital, a fancy box of cigars. Then, in March and April of 1918, he shot down 17 more airplanes. His total was now 80.

On the morning of April 21, 1918, a flight of 15 British fighters encountered the Flying Circus. A huge aerial battle ensued, and during the confusion, a young Canadian pilot, Lieutenant Wilford May, realized that he had, right behind him, a scarlet airplane. The Red Baron! Lieutenant May was very inexperienced; frightened now, he took his plane lower and lower, twisting and looping, trying to shake the red plane off his tail. Seeing the danger he was in, his Captain, Roy Brown, came swooping down, firing his guns. On the ground, as the three planes flew just above their heads, a group of Australian gunners began firing their guns as well. Suddenly, the red plane dived and crashed in the middle of an area that the Australians had been holding for days. Quickly, some Australian soldiers ran to the downed plane and discovered, to their astonishment, that Manfred was inside, lifeless. Neither the two fighter pilots nor the Australian gunners could be sure who had brought down the Red Baron.

The British officer who was in charge of that region, Major Blake, took responsibility for Manfred's burial. Like most of the Allies' air officers, he regarded the Red Baron with the utmost respect, and he organized a full military funeral with honors. Even though Manfred had been their enemy, the British buried him as if he were a brother. On his grave they laid a beautiful wreath adorned with these words: "To Our Gallant and Worthy Foe."

This is how a man can be a hero even to his enemies, by conducting his life with honor even in the midst of battle. Manfred von Richthoven was such a man, and all who knew him celebrated him for it.

Chapter 15

The Last Journey of the *Lusitania*

On a bright May morning in 1915, Pier 54 in New York City bustled with activity. Motorcars and horse-drawn carriages thronged the dockside, while porters laden with heavy boxes and carts piled with trunks struggled to push their way through the crowds of people. Looming high above the hustle and noise, the British ocean liner *Lusitania* lay quietly docked, readying herself for another journey across the Atlantic. Although she was the focus of the frantic scurrying below, she was a serene and beautiful sight, a graceful ship distinguished by her huge size, her four symmetrical smokestacks, and her reputation for awesome speed. Why, the *Lusitania* could make the ocean crossing in only five days!

Many of the passengers boarding the ship that morning had chosen the *Lusitania* for their journey precisely because of her fabled speed. Another ship, an American liner called the *New York,* was due to leave the harbor just ahead of the *Lusitania* and sail to the same destination, but she was not as fast, and so many had chosen the English ship instead.

For some, the choice of the *Lusitania* had less to do with speed and more to do with luxury. The *Lusy* boasted the best accommodations at sea, from her fabulously decorated first-class dining room, which was modeled after a French palace, to the sturdy and comfortable bunks down in the third-class cabins.

There was no more comfortable ship upon which to travel, and for some, that was the only consideration.

But the speed and luxury of the *Lusitania* did not come without risk. Since 1914 the United Kingdom, under whose flag the ship sailed, had been at war with Germany, and one of the Germans' many strategies of war involved the sinking of ships with submarines. At first the deadly submarines had attacked only naval warships, but by 1915 the Germans had begun to sink merchant vessels as well. Any ship who ventured into a submarine's hunting site was fair game to the Germans, and in February of 1915, Germany declared all of the seas around Great Britain to be a war zone: any ship could be sunk without warning. Just that very morning, a grim warning from the German Embassy had been printed in every newspaper in New York City. If you choose to sail aboard an English ship, it said, you put yourself in danger. "Travelers sailing in the war zone on the ships of Great Britain or her allies do so at their own risk."

The *Lusitania's* captain, William Turner, tried to calm the passengers' fears. When reporters from the New York newspapers asked him about the German warning, he scoffed. "The *Lusitania* is too fast to be caught by a submarine," he said confidently. "She will be safe."

And so, despite the German warning, only a few nervous souls had cancelled their passage. When the *Lusitania* left New York City that morning, she would be carrying 1,265 passengers and a crew of 694.

As eighteen-year-old nurse Alice Lines followed her employers up the gangplank to the first-class staterooms in the middle of the ship, she could spare only a hurried glance at the *Lusitania's* enormous hull. All of her attention was focused on her two charges: three-month-old Audrey Pearl and five-year-old Stuart. Warren and Amy Pearl, the children's parents, strolled ahead of Alice, nodding gracefully to acquaintances and commenting on the luxurious surroundings of the first-class accommodations.

Behind Alice, another nurse, Greta Lorenson, held three-year-old Amy Pearl firmly by one hand while balancing two-year-old Susan on her hip.

Alice was looking forward to the voyage. Her employers were a warm, considerate couple, and the children were dear to her. She knew that, as first-class passengers, they would have the best of everything: delicious food, lovely staterooms with exquisite furniture and linens, and stewards from the ship to see to their every need. She thought for a moment of the humble people down in third class, deep in the bowels of the ship. Even there, though, the *Lusitania* offered good meals and comfortable rooms and a pleasant journey for all. For a few days, perhaps, the passengers could enjoy their holiday and forget for a little while the dreadful war in Europe. For Alice and the two hundred other Americans aboard the ship, the war seemed only a distant thunder. Their nation was neutral and not involved in the conflict. For the Europeans, though, the war was an ever-present specter, haunting even the hallways of this elegant ship. But for all of the passengers, the war was closer than they realized. Down in her cargo holds, the *Lusitania* carried a large shipment of mortar shells, bombs made in American factories to be used by the British army in its fight against Germany. Because of her speed, she had been secretly carrying desperately-needed weapons and bombs for the British for many months.

Shortly before noon, as Alice was settling the children in their stateroom, the *Lusitania* slipped away from the docks and steamed down the Hudson River. As she entered the waters of the Atlantic, no one on board knew that she would never see New York again.

For four days the ship glided easily across the gray Atlantic. The passengers ate and slept, danced in the elegant ballroom, and played shuffleboard games on the teak deck. It was an easy, luxurious journey.

While the ship steamed toward England, though, other

ships were also on the move.

Below the cold waters of the Irish Sea, a German submarine, the U-20, stalked back and forth like a wolf. She was captained by a young officer named Walter Schwieger. Like all of Germany's submarine commanders, he had been ordered to sink every merchant ship he could, without warning. On May 5th U-20 sank a British schooner, a sailing vessel named the *Earl of Latham,* whose cargo hold was packed to the brim with bacon, eggs, and potatoes. That same day Captain Schwieger fired a torpedo at another ship and barely missed it. Then on May 6th, the submarine sank two more British steamers. Satisfied with his accomplishments so far, the captain submerged his ship and headed further out to sea. U-20 was low on fuel and had only three torpedoes remaining, but, nonetheless, her captain decided to wait for another day or two before turning back toward Germany. He hoped to catch another ship, and so U-20 lingered, silent in the cold waters.

On the evening of May 6th, Captain Turner received a radio message: "Submarines active off the south coast of Ireland." Since this was exactly where the *Lusitania* was headed, the captain took every precaution he could. He closed all the watertight doors on the ship and ordered twice as many lookouts to be posted. He commanded the crew to put the ship on blackout, which means that they covered up all of the portholes and extinguished any outside lights. Lifeboats were swung out over the sides of the ship, so that they could be lowered at a moment's notice. Then, having done all that he could, the captain set off to attend a concert in the first-class lounge. During the intermission he stood and addressed the audience. He told them about the submarine warning but assured them again of the *Lusitania*'s speed. No ship going faster than 15 knots has ever been attacked, he reminded them. And he intended to steam toward Ireland with the engines at full power.

The passengers could not help being frightened, though. Many among them began to make their own plans in case the unthinkable happened. Some passengers decided to sleep up on deck that night, buckled into their life jackets. Warren Pearl took Alice Lines aside, and spoke gravely to her. "If the ship is attacked, you must take the children to the deck at once and look for a lifeboat. Do not wait for my wife and me; we will find you on deck. Do you know where the lifejackets are?"

Alice nodded. "In the stateroom closet."

Her employer smiled. "I am sure all will be well. But it's best to be prepared."

The morning of May 7th dawned gray and foggy. Anxious passengers lined the ship's rails, listening to the mournful call of her foghorn and murmuring uneasily about how slowly she was moving. When the misty fog began to lift about midmorning, a wave of relief swept over the ship. Far away along the horizon, a green line of land appeared above the ocean's calm surface: Ireland. Just the sight of their destination made the passengers feel safe again, and they sat down to their noonday meal to eat with renewed appetite.

They did not know that only a short distance away, U-20 lurked just under the surface of the sea. Her lookouts had spotted the *Lusitania*'s distinctive four smokestacks when she had emerged out of the fog, and they had been waiting patiently as she drew ever more near. They could hardly believe their good fortune; here was Britain's most celebrated ship, far too fast for them to ever catch, and she was sailing right into their sights!

At 2:10 P.M. the *Lusitania* was only seven hundred yards away. Captain Schwieger ordered his gunner to fire one of their last torpedoes.

On board the ship, a lookout was horrified to see the streaming bubbles aiming directly toward them. "Torpedoes coming!" he shouted over and over. Captain Turner heard his cries, but it was too late. The torpedo struck the ship and exploded just below the waterline. Within just a few moments, a second giant explosion rocked the ship as the secret cargo of mortar shells in the hold caught fire.

At once the ship began to sink. Frantic passengers ran for the lifeboats in a swirling confusion of men, women, and children. In the first-class stateroom, Alice Lines hurried to bundle baby Audrey and little Stuart into their lifejackets. Stuart was crying, but Alice comforted him. "Hang on to me whatever happens," she told him.

Carefully she tied Audrey to her chest with a woolen shawl, and then, taking a firm hold of Stuart's hand, she said, "Come along, we won't wait for anything."

Coming out on deck into the mass of people, she struggled to hang on to the children, but she pushed forward until she managed to reach a lifeboat. A crewman quickly lifted Stuart and handed him across the ship's rail to the people already in the boat, but then he shook his head at Alice.

"This boat is full," he shouted.

Alice was terrified. She could not let Stuart go alone! The lifeboat was being lowered; soon he would be out of reach. Gathering her courage, the young nurse leaped out over the rail, clutching little Audrey in her arms. She splashed into the water beside the lifeboat and almost instantly felt the cold water sapping her strength. But her long auburn hair floated out behind her, and the people on the boat grabbed it and pulled her and the baby on board. Quickly she gathered Stuart into her arms as well, and then looked back. The ship was gone. It had been only eighteen minutes since the torpedo had struck.

For the survivors, a desperate wait began for someone to come and rescue them. Most of them had been separated from their loved ones and did not know if they were alive or dead. Huddled in the lifeboat, Alice worried frantically about the rest of the Pearl family. Had they escaped the sinking ship?

Other ships, having heard the *Lusitania*'s final distress call, steamed, sailed, and rowed at full speed toward the site of the disaster. There they began to pull survivors off the lifeboats, and some out of the ocean's waters as well. Alice and the two children were picked up by a government patrol boat, which carried them to the nearest town, the Irish city Queenstown.

All that day and through the night, Warren Pearl frantically searched for his wife and children. He found his wife, at last, rescued by a tramp steamer. Together they heard that a young woman matching Alice's description was being cared for by some kind local people. They rushed to the house and rejoiced to find Alice and Audrey and Stuart, even while they grieved that Amy and Susan and their nurse Greta had not been found.

Many families lost someone that day. Of the 1,265 passengers, 785 were killed. 413 members of the crew lost their lives as well.

The entire world was shocked and horrified to hear of Germany's attack on the *Lusitania*, an unarmed passenger ship. World leaders sent angry letters to the German government, demanding that it stop using submarines in this way. The president of the United States, Woodrow Wilson, wept when he heard the news, and asked, "How can any nation calling itself civilized do such a horrible thing?"

For a little while, Germany kept its submarines at home and did not use them. But just a year later, desperate to win the war, she sent the U-boats out again with orders to sink every ship they found. And this so angered the people and the leaders of the United States that, in 1917, the Americans declared war on Germany, a war in which they would ultimately prevail.

In sinking the *Lusitania*, Germany sank her own chances for victory in the Great War.

Chapter 16

The Russian Revolution

As the Great War lingered on and on, gobbling up ever larger quantities of men and machines, medicine and materials, the people who lived in these warring nations began to suffer. Little food was available, especially in the large cities, and the peasants and farmers who lived and worked out in the countryside were angry and exhausted, and sorrowful beyond measure as they saw entire villages emptied of their young men, who were sent off to fight, and their harvests, which were taken to feed the armies. All of Europe was covered with the gloomy smoke of war.

This was especially true in the large nation of Russia. If you will take a moment to look at your globe or a map of the world, you will find Russia to the east of Europe and north of China. You can see that it is very large indeed, a huge country filled with trackless forests and high, cold plains. It is adorned with some noble, bustling cities, places like Moscow and St. Petersburg, and a great deal of open, empty space dotted with scattered farms and tiny villages. At the beginning of the twentieth century, there were large portions of Russia that had changed very little since the Middle Ages.

In the year 1916, though, a bitter wind had begun to blow through the farms and villages and cities. The common people in the cities, factory workers and shopkeepers, were furiously angry.

Their lives were difficult, with long hours spent at work; poor, drafty houses with no plumbing or heat; very little pay for the work they were doing; and dangerous conditions in the factories, where deadly accidents happened every day. Out in the countryside, the farmers and butchers and dairymen were no happier: they were required to pay huge sums of money to the government in order to have the right to work the land. And as the war continued, food became scarce. In the city of St. Petersburg, or Petrograd as it was called then, many shops closed early each day or did not open at all, because there was no bread, no sugar, no meat or tea to sell. The shops that did receive a few provisions were instantly besieged with long, long lines of people trying to buy what little they could. By October of 1916, the police sent a report to the leaders of Russia warning that "the lower classes of the empire are enraged by the burdens of daily existence."

The leader of Russia, its king so to speak, was a man called the tsar. His name was Nicholas II, and he was a member of the Romanov family, who had been ruling Russia for many years. Nicholas governed Russia with a strict hand and viewed himself as a father to his country, a father whose commands could not be questioned and whose law was absolute. He believed firmly that the people of Russia were completely devoted to him, and so he did not take very seriously the cries for change that were erupting from his suffering people.

At the beginning of February, in 1917, the common workers of Petrograd began a strike. I wonder if my readers have heard of a strike before. A strike means that the people refused to go to their jobs, instead marching through the city streets shouting and singing, demanding better pay and better living conditions. By March 10th every shop and factory, every school and office had been shut down. The entire city was at a standstill with the workers filling the streets and attending public meetings, which quickly became loud storms of shouting, angry people.

Alarmed, the tsar ordered the army to break up the crowds,

using even their guns if needed. But the soldiers were reluctant; they themselves were angry and hungry, exhausted from the bitter battles of the Great War, and worried for their families. They began to mutiny, which means they disobeyed the order they were given. Many of them joined the rioting crowds of striking workers.

All over the city, pictures and statues of the tsar were torn down and trampled. The city was a mass of confusion, and all forms of authority disappeared. Trying to gain a little control, some of the workers organized themselves into a group called a soviet, to speak for the crowds of angry people.

These particular workers of the Petrograd Soviet believed firmly in a way of living called socialism. They were followers of the writings of a man named Karl Marx. He thought that everything in a country—all the farms, shops, factories, and offices—should be owned, not by individual farmers and shopkeepers, but by all the citizens of that country all at once. The food and supplies that the farms and shops and factories produce should then be shared by everyone together, with each person working and receiving the same amount as each other person. In socialism, there are no owners and no bosses, only workers.

These socialists had been living and meeting in Petrograd for many years, trying to convince others to join with them. Now they saw their chance to influence many more people. The Petrograd Soviet claimed loudly that it was speaking for all of Russia's workers.

Realizing, too late, how deep this problem had grown, Nicholas took a train to Petrograd to take command of the city himself. But when he arrived, the chiefs of his army and the few remaining members of his government insisted that he must give up his throne and crown. It was the only way to quell the furious anger of the crowds. And so, on March 15th the tsar became merely Nicholas Romanov. The rule of Russia passed into the hands of a committee led by a socialist named Alexander Kerensky.

Now, there lived in Switzerland, far from the angry streets of

Petrograd, an exiled Russian socialist named Vladimir Lenin. He was a leader of a certain group of socialists who called themselves the Bolshevik Party. *Bolshevik* means "a minority." These were men who believed in the strongest possible form of socialism, called Marxism after Karl Marx, where no one owned anything, not even their homes or clothing. They had broken away from the majority of Russian socialists back in 1903 amongst many bitter arguments, and Lenin had been forced to leave Russia.

In April of 1917 he made his way back to Petrograd. It might have been a dangerous journey, crossing through the battlefields of Germany, except that the Germans were happy to let him through unharmed. They knew who he was and what he believed, and they thought, rather craftily, that Lenin's return to his homeland would only cause more trouble and instability in Russia, and since Russia was their enemy, any trouble there could only be a good thing for Germany. But they would let Lenin pass through Germany only in a sealed train. They did not want this man starting a revolution in their own country.

Lenin perceived that the time had come for him to lead a Marxist revolution in Russia, a complete overthrow of all the established forms of government with the goal of making Russia a thoroughly socialist nation. He began to give fiery speeches throughout the city, attracting huge crowds, calling for "all power to the Soviets." The popularity of the Bolshevik party grew and grew among the city's common people. But Lenin had no real power, and the leaders of the government watched him with suspicion. Eventually, they threatened to arrest him, and he had to flee to Finland.

Unfortunately, the huge crowds of workers were beginning to view the new government with just as much distaste as they had viewed the tsar only a few months before. The Great War was still grinding on, there was still no food, the factories were still dirty and unsafe. Nothing had really changed. They saw the Marxist Bolsheviks as the only hope for change. By October of

1917 Lenin realized that the government could pose no real threat to him, because his popularity with the workers was so great. He returned to the city. On November 3rd, he wrote a proclamation insisting that the government be eliminated and the Petersburg Soviet be put in charge of all Russia.

Then, on November 7th, Lenin led his revolutionaries into battle against the government. Soldiers who had abandoned the army and joined with the Bolsheviks attacked all of the important buildings in Petrograd, especially the Winter Palace where the government did its business. By 2:00 A.M. the next morning, they had seized all power in the city, and Alexander Kerensky, the leader of the conquered government, fled.

On November 8th Lenin established his Marxist government. All of Russia would be ruled by soviets, local groups of workers who would rule over each town. At first, Lenin insisted grandly that the members of these soviets would be freely elected. Russia would be "a worker's Paradise." But then it became clear to him that, while he had a great deal of support in Petrograd and the other large cities, the people out in the countryside did not trust him or the other Bolsheviks at all. So he declared that only members of the Bolshevik party could be part of the soviets.

Lenin now turned his attentions to Russia's terrible problems. He arranged a treaty with Germany so that Russia was no longer a part of the Great War. And to keep his army fed and maintain his support in the cities, he forced the farmers out in the countryside to give their harvests to the starving cities for little money.

Many in Russia were horrified by the prospect of living in a socialist nation. They looked back unhappily to the days of the tsar. In 1918, they formed a "White Army" and declared war upon the "Red Army" of the Bolsheviks. Soon, all of Russia was plunged into a civil war between white and red that lasted for three years. Millions of Russians suffered terribly, whether they believed in Lenin or not, a suffering made all the more fierce by a great famine that struck all of Russia in 1921.

By 1922 Lenin was very sick, and he was also very worried. A new leader had risen in the Bolshevik Party, a man named Joseph Stalin. He was already very powerful in Russia, and Lenin cautioned his fellow socialists to be careful. "His unlimited authority is unacceptable," he said. "I urge my comrades to think about a way of removing Stalin. He is unnecessarily rough and rude, flaws that are intolerable in a leader."

In January of 1924, Lenin died. For four days his body lay in state, and 900,000 Russian mourners passed by it.

In England, a great man named Winston Churchill, who would become all the more great in just a few years, spoke of Lenin's death with regret. He had urged his nation and others to intervene in the Russian Revolution and destroy the Marxist Bolsheviks. He hated all that Lenin stood for. Yet, he said, "Now the Russian people are left floundering in a bog. Their worst misfortune was his birth. Their next worst was his death."

Why would he speak such words? Because he was looking upon the Russia that was left—the suffering, ruined Russia, whose only remaining leader was that rough and rude Joseph Stalin.

About him, and about Winston Churchill, you will soon learn much more.

Chapter 17

The Great Depression

Imagine with me a small boy, playing in an open field. His mother and father are off in the distance, setting out a picnic under a shade tree. "Be careful!" his mother calls after him, but he is filled with reckless excitement and does not hear her words. Instead he runs and jumps, thrilled to have all this wide new space to explore. Before long he has found a long stick, and he is having a grand game of knights in armor, with the stick as his sword and tall daisies as foes. He runs more quickly and jumps more wildly, with no thought at all for the placement of his feet. And so, when he trips and falls, he falls hard, tearing his pants' leg and scraping his knee. As his mother picks him up and comforts him, she tells him gently, "You must look where you are going."

The world in the 1920s was just like that little boy. The terrible Great War had ended, and people everywhere were filled with a giddy excitement and a new confidence. Inventions such as the automobile and radio made anything seem possible. The future beckoned brightly, and the world was filled with such energy and excitement that this time in history is called the Roaring Twenties.

It was in the spirit of this happy optimism that people began to take their money and invest it into the stock market.

Those of you who remember reading about Ferdinand de Lessops, the French engineer who built the Suez Canal, may recall how he got the money for that large project. He sold shares, which meant that, for a sum of money, a person could own a tiny portion of the Canal and then be paid back plus a little extra. A stock is like that; it is a share of a company. Suppose that you are a businessman; perhaps you own a company that makes baseball bats. You would like to expand your factory so that you can make many more baseball bats each day, but you need money to build that larger factory. So you sell stock in your company: you offer ordinary people the opportunity to own a tiny portion of your company, and each year you will then give each of your stockholders a tiny portion of the money that the company makes, its profit. That payment is called a dividend. This plan works well; you sell lots of stock and raise plenty of money to build a fine new factory, which then produces millions of baseball bats. As the bats are sold, your company makes a large profit, part of which you then pay back to your stockholders as dividends, and everyone is happy.

It sounds wonderful, doesn't it? Are some of you asking your father right now if you may take your money out of your piggy bank and invest it in stocks?

But wait! What if the baseball bats do not sell? What if the people who shop in the stores all decide to buy soccer balls instead? The baseball bat company does not sell enough bats to make a profit, and what happens then to the stockholders? They do not get their dividends, and if things go very badly with the company and it goes out of business, the stockholders will lose all the money they originally gave the company. That is the risk of buying stocks. Do you still want to take all your money out of your piggy bank?

Well, as I am sure you can guess, the stock market is the place where stocks from many different companies are bought and sold. Each nation has its own stock market, and when people buy stocks there, they are said to be investing, with the idea that they will receive the dividends that the companies will pay.

In the 1920s, more and more people invested their money

in the stock market. Stock prices began to rise, and newspapers carried stories about common, humble people who bought stocks and then sold them and became fabulously wealthy. This only encouraged more investment. People who had previously kept all of their money in a bank, or at home in a jar in the closet, began to take every penny they could find and use it to buy stocks.

The profits seemed to be a sure thing. Soon even large companies were taking their savings and investing them. Banks began taking their customers' money and putting it in the stock market. Some people, even very wealthy people, borrowed money from banks or from their own businesses to invest.

There were warning signs. Factories were not producing as many items to sell; carpenters were not building many new houses; mines were not digging out as much ore. But just like the little boy in the beginning of our story, most of the world charged merrily onward, heedless of the danger of such reckless excitement.

And then, suddenly, on the morning of Thursday, October 24, 1929, prices in the American stock market in New York City began to go down. Even today, no one knows for sure why. Perhaps it started with just a few people wanting to sell the stock they owned, and then others noticed them selling and began to sell their own stock. Prices went lower and lower. Like a snowball rolling down a hill, the number of sellers grew larger and larger, so large that people began to panic, fearfully trying to sell their stock before its prices fell further. A group of bankers saw what was happening and quelled the panic by investing a large sum of their own money in the stock market. The prices stopped falling; everyone breathed a sigh of relief.

But it was only a temporary calm. On October 29th, a date that has been forever after known as Black Tuesday, the prices of stocks began to fall once more, and this time no one could stop them. People were desperate to sell before they lost every penny they had invested, but because everyone was selling, no one was buying. Fear and desperation spread. People realized that the banks which held their money had put that money in the stock market, which was now failing. They ran to the banks, demanding their money, but the banks had no money to give. The money was all gone, buried under the avalanche of falling stock prices.

The prices in the stock market continued to fall for days, until November 23, 1929. By then most people had no money left. Many companies were ruined and had to stop doing business. People's faith in banks had been destroyed.

Companies that stayed in business had nevertheless lost much of their money, and could no longer afford to pay their workers as much as they had before. They began to cut the workers' pay or offer them fewer hours to work. And so, of course, those same workers then had much less money of their own to spend at the food market or the drug store, and then those businesses as well began to fail. And as businesses closed their doors, more and more workers were left without a job of any kind.

This kind of situation, where millions of people have lost their jobs, where banks have failed and factories are producing little, is called a depression. This depression, of course, was not confined only to the United States. From 1929 until 1939 the entire world was shadowed by what is now called the Great Depression.

Even before the disaster of Black Tuesday struck in New York City, other nations were already teetering on the brink of depression, and some had long since fallen into it. The Great War had plunged both Germany and Russia into deep poverty; while the rest of the world roared wildly through the 1920s, the people of those nations were struggling daily just to buy a loaf of bread. By 1929, when the American stock market suffered its thundering crash, the other nations of the world were already weakened by careless investing, crushing debts, and silent factories. Their stock markets began to fail too, and one by one, each nation in Europe faced its own "Black Tuesday." Businesses closed, having lost all of their money; workers were turned away, since there were no jobs to be had; families endured great hardship, doing their best to live with very little. Americans and Europeans stopped buying products from other countries, and so those countries, in places like South America and Asia, fell into depressions as well.

All over the world, frightened and angry people began to demand that their leaders find a way out of this terrible situation. But a depression is not a problem that is easily solved. Leaders around the world did what they could. In the United States, the American president Franklin Roosevelt used the government's money to provide help for poor and homeless people, and also gave many men jobs building things for the nation itself, such as dams or bridges. Nations in Europe tried to follow Roosevelt's lead and start the same sort of government programs, but they often couldn't agree on what exactly to do, and bitter arguments in Spain and Great Britain and France led to governments deeply divided, with leaders removed from office and new ones elected who were powerless to provide any solutions.

As 1940 came and went, however, the shadow of the Depression finally began to lift, but not because of the efforts of world leaders or the return of the Roaring Twenties' reckless excitement. No, the Depression was vanquished by the overshadowing of an even greater darkness: the Second World War. And that is a story for the chapters to come.

Chapter 18

The *Hindenberg*

N ow I will tell you of a man in Germany who had a dream, and what became of that dream in America.

In 1928, when this story begins, it was not easy to be a German. The country had been on the losing side of the Great War, and the victors in that war blamed the Germans for causing it in the first place. As punishment, the winners of the war were requiring the Germans to pay reparations; they must give huge amounts of money to the countries that Germany had attacked during the war. These payments were making the German nation and people poor and desperate. Through the whole country ran a grim spirit of resentment towards the war's victorious nations, and when the Great Depression settled over them, making their lives even more difficult, that resentment turned to anger.

A man named Adolf Hitler saw this anger as a way to gain power. He began to give speeches at loud rallies, urging the German people to rise up again, to be proud of their warlike heritage and shake off the losses of the Great War and the Depression. He blamed others for the Germans' problems and shook his fist at the rest of the world. Many Germans gathered to hear him and began to join him. His group came to be called the Nazi Party, and it grew more and more powerful.

But there were many Germans who looked with dismay upon the Nazis' bluster. One of these was a man named Hugo Eckener, who dreamed of bringing people together, not through anger and misplaced pride, but through flight, lighter than air. You see, Hugo Eckener was a man who built airships, and he saw in them a way to heal the wounds of war.

An airship is a flying machine that looks like something out of a dream. Can you imagine with me? See in your mind's eye a giant cloth bag, much bigger than a house, filled with hydrogen gas, which is lighter than air so that the bag floats effortlessly upward, like a helium-filled balloon at a child's birthday party. Now, imagine six or eight of these giant bags, all tethered together and contained inside a huge cylinder-shaped cage. A smooth covering of sleek, metallic cloth covers the cage, so that the entire machine looks like a gigantic silver whale, hovering above the ground. Underneath its belly, a compartment called a gondola holds the passengers, and at either side, large engines fitted with two propellers each move the whole wondrous contraption forward through the air. At its tail, the airship has a giant fin, so that it can be steered by a pilot within the gondola. In flight, the airship moves with silent grace, so steady that passengers inside the gondola have to look out the windows to confirm that they are actually moving. Flying in an airship is almost magical.

Hugo Eckener was the president of the German company that built these wonderful machines. The Germans called them "zeppelins," after the name of the German nobleman who had originally invented them thirty years before. This man, Count Ferdinand von Zeppelin, had imagined his airships carrying, not peaceful passengers, but deadly bombs. And, in fact, the silent zeppelins had been used to attack the city of London during the Great War. The people of London had never heard them coming.

Now that the Great War was over, Hugo Eckener wanted to use his airships for a very different purpose. He knew that nothing promoted good will and understanding between people of different nations more than travel. But travel between the Americas and Europe was a slow, rather difficult thing; it meant a journey by ship that would take two weeks or more. What if, instead, passengers could travel from Berlin to New York City in only three days, floating lighter than air in the luxurious gondola of a zeppelin? Would not such an opportunity encourage much more travel between the two continents? Hugo Eckener believed that it would, and that such travel would lead to much more openness and friendship between Germany and the rest of the world.

With that dream in mind, Hugo and his company had constructed a new, fabulous airship, the largest ever. It was called the *Graf Zeppelin*, and in 1929, Hugo proposed to fly it all the way around the globe, captaining the flight himself and doing everything he could along the way to promote travel and good will between Germany and other countries. First though, he flew the *Graf Zeppelin* across the Atlantic and landed it in New York. The Americans were thrilled; they threw a parade for Eckener along the streets of New York City.

The worldwide flight in 1929 was a huge success. Hugo landed the ship in dozens of different locations, everywhere drawing crowds of wildly cheering spectators. The president of the United States, Herbert Hoover, compared Hugo to "a great adventurer, like Columbus or Magellan." But Hugo disagreed. He was not a hero, he said. He merely wished "to be of service to mankind in the development of air travel."

By 1931 the *Graf Zeppelin* was making regular trips across the Atlantic. Satisfied, Hugo turned to his next plan: he wished to make an even greater airship, larger, more luxurious, more advanced. At his factory in Germany, he built a gigantic hangar and began assembling the new ship. First, his workers constructed huge metal rings and then hung them from the ceiling of the hangar in a long row. Then, long metal strips were attached to the rings, connecting them all together in a cylinder. The enormous balloons that would contain the hydrogen gas were inserted inside. Cotton fabric was stretched over it all to make a skin, and then the skin was coated with shiny metallic paint. Finally, the gondola and the engines were attached, and the new airship was ready to take flight. It only needed a name.

By this time, the Nazi party was completely in control of Germany. They had been watching Hugo's work with greedy eyes; they knew that this fabulous zeppelin could be a powerful tool in their hands. When the airship was almost finished, they sent a message to Hugo: would it not be a noble and wonderful idea to name this new ship the *Adolf Hitler*, after their great leader?

But, as you will remember, Hugo disliked and distrusted the Nazis. In fact, in the election that had just passed, he had intended to run for president of Germany against Hitler and had only decided not to because of his passion for his work. He certainly would not be naming his lovely ship after a man whom he considered evil! He sent back to them a stiff reply: the ship would be called the *Hindenberg*, for a famous German general.

The Nazi leaders were incredulous. How could this man defy them? Again they sent a message, more strongly worded this time. They demanded that Hugo allow them to use the *Hindenberg*'s giant hangar for a political rally. He should be very honored, they insisted. The great Hitler himself was coming to give a speech at the rally! But again Hugo refused. No Nazis would be giving speeches in his hangar!

Now the Nazis considered Hugo an enemy. They wanted to arrest him and throw him in prison, as they had done with so many others who had opposed them, but his international fame prevented it. Instead, they removed him from leadership in his company and refused to allow his name to be attached to any of his achievements. When newspapers praised the beauty and luxury of the *Hindenberg*, they never mentioned its creator. And when the *Hindenberg* set out for the United States in May of 1936, Hugo Eckener was not aboard.

That year, the graceful airship made nine flights across the ocean. When it floated silently over New York City, the people below would fill the rooftops and streets, awestruck. As amazing as the *Graf Zeppelin* had been, the *Hindenberg* was all the greater.

Even though he had been sidelined from his own company, Hugo was still involved in the business of airships. He struck a deal with an American company to build two giant zeppelins in America, and he made plans to build two more in Germany. Soon, anyone who could afford a ticket would be soaring over the Atlantic on an airship. His dream of travel between nations was coming true.

A year later, in May of 1937, the *Hindenberg* set out for America again, on the first of twelve planned trips that year. She carried 36 wealthy passengers and a crew of 61. After a three-day ocean crossing, she floated toward her landing field in New Jersey. Thunderstorms were blackening the sky all around, so the airship cruised in lazy circles over Manhattan and the Atlantic coastline for a few hours, waiting for a window of opportunity to land. Finally, six hours behind schedule, the captain decided to try a landing at about seven o'clock in the evening. The ship slowed to a stop and hovered above the landing field, and the crew dropped the mooring rope so that the ship could be secured. All seemed well.

And then the *Hindenberg* exploded. In less than one minute, the beautiful ship was a mass of flame.

The ship had been near enough to the ground that many of the people aboard were able to escape; some 67 of them survived. But the *Hindenberg* was dead, completely destroyed; only the metal skeleton was recognizable amongst the ashy wreckage.

That morning Hugo Eckener was awakened by a somber telephone call. The *Hindenberg* was no more, and Hugo knew that his dream was dead, as well. No one would want to build any more airships after such a disaster.

The cause of the explosion has never been discovered, but Hugo himself came to believe that the pilot had turned the ship too roughly when entering the landing field, causing one of the balloons inside the ship to rupture and the hydrogen gas to leak out. When hydrogen mixes with air, it becomes very flammable, and with the thunderstorms in the area, it would have needed only one tiny spark of static electricity to cause the deadly explosion.

As reasonable as this explanation sounded, Hugo was nevertheless correct in his guess that no one would any longer wish to ride in an airship. But even with this disaster, and the continued power of Adolf Hitler and the Nazis in Germany, Hugo was not wholly discouraged. He had turned his eye to another form of travel: the airplane. He believed that with the airplane, his dream of open travel would not die. And he was right.

But first, something would have to be done about Hitler and the Nazis. That was a grim task that other men and women would face.

Chapter 19

Chain Home

In 1915, amidst the storm of the Great War, a young man
named Robert Watson-Watt approached the War Office
in London, England. He was lately come from Scotland, where
he had been assistant and star pupil of a physics professor at the
University of Dundee, and where he had become an expert in the
new technology of radio. Now he had left his green native land
and traveled to London's gray towers. He wished to be of service
in the war effort, and he wanted to offer his knowledge of radio.

But the War Office had no jobs available just then that
would suit Robert's education and skills. So instead, he went to
the Meteorological Office, where all the weathermen worked,
and offered himself to them instead. "I have some ideas about
radio," he told them. "What if we could use radio waves to detect
thunderstorms, and then warn approaching pilots so that they are
not caught by surprise?" The weathermen were very interested,
and they put Robert to work.

I hope that you remember, from our story about radio, that
radio waves are electromagnetic. And of course you know that
the lightning strikes created by a thunderstorm are huge bolts
of electricity. When lightning flashes, it gives off radio waves.
Knowing this, Robert Watson-Watt built a receiver to listen for
these waves, and he was immediately successful. He could detect
storms from miles away, but, unfortunately, his simple receiver

had no way of indicating the direction of the storm. Robert solved this problem by building an antenna that could turn in a complete circle. The signal from the storm would grow stronger as the antenna turned toward it, and then fade as the antenna turned away. In this way, Robert could tell from which direction the radio waves were coming, and pilots could be warned of the storm in their path.

Once Robert had figured all of this out, he also needed a way to make the signal visible, so that an operator could easily see and understand it. To do this, Robert attached a special machine to his antenna, a device called an oscilloscope. This little machine is a box with a screen, which takes the electrical radio signal and shows it as a picture of a moving wave. The bigger the wave gets on the screen, the stronger the signal coming to the antenna. Now any worker could be trained to look at the screen, check the direction of the signal, and then give the warning to any airplanes in that area. Robert's new thunderstorm detection system was a success, and by 1923 it was being used regularly.

In 1927 the English government set up a new Radio Research Station and asked Robert to be its leader. By this time, Robert was working to make his radio detection system more accurate; it needed to be able to find objects much smaller than thunderstorms, and it needed to be able to tell not only the direction of an object but also how far away that object might be. To do this, Robert and his fellow scientists were using radio waves in a different way. They were shooting the waves from a transmitter in short, fierce pulses. The radio waves would then bounce off an oncoming object and echo back to an antenna. The scientists would measure the time it took from the instant the waves left the transmitter until the echo returned and use that measurement to figure out how far away the object was.

Meanwhile, as Robert worked quietly in his Research Station, clouds of fear and unease were gathering. Anxiously, many in England watched as Adolf Hitler and his Nazi government stormed into power. They listened to his angry speeches. They watched as he built up Germany's army, even though he was forbidden to do so by the treaty that had ended the Great War. They knew in their hearts that he would not be content to stay within his own borders in Germany. It was only a matter of time before he unleashed war once more in Europe. So, in 1934, the British Royal Air Force came to Robert to talk about the problem of air defense.

The Air Force was worried, and rightly so. During the Great War, the Germans had used their ghostly airships to bomb London. Twenty times the airships had soared over the city, bearing their deadly loads, and twenty times the Air Force had scrambled pilots to meet them, but always the pilots failed. Despite their huge size, these German zeppelins were silent, and so the British fighter pilots trying to defend their city had been unable to find them in the dark skies.

Even worse, in the twenty years since World War I had ended, the Germans had greatly improved their airplanes. Now German bombers could fly so high that British guns on the ground could not reach them, and by the time British fighter pilots could find them in the air, the enemy pilots would have already dropped their bombs and be racing back home. There was no way to know when enemy airplanes were coming until it was too late.

A solution was desperately needed. There must be a way to see the enemy airships and bombers before they reached their targets. Could Robert's radio detection help?

Robert was certain that it could. On February 12, 1935, he sent a secret message to the Air Force, with the title "Detection and Location of Aircraft by Radio Methods." He showed exactly how the signal would be reflected from the airplane and measured, and how he could develop a direction-finder that could also show how high the plane was flying. The Air Force was hopeful after reading this report, but before giving Robert permission and money to begin working on this project, they asked him to prove to them that radio waves could detect a flying aircraft. So, on February

26th, Robert performed a demonstration. It was such a secret that only Robert, an assistant, and one man from the Air Force were present. Robert had set up the radio antenna and arranged for a British bomber to be flown nearby. As the plane soared past, the signal showed clearly on the oscilloscope screen, and the radio pulses revealed its distance. The system worked!

The British Prime Minister himself was informed of the test's success, and Robert was given permission to work solely on this project. In May of 1935, a small troop of Robert's assistants secretly left the Radio Research Station. They traveled across England to a lonely peninsula on the coast of the North Sea and set up their equipment in a group of old Air Force buildings battered by the cold winds. By June they were detecting aircraft ten miles away, and by the end of the year, under Robert's direction, they were finding planes that were sixty miles away. British officials were impressed, and so they were ready to listen as Robert explained his ideas for using radio detection to protect the lives of Englishmen. Plans were made to set up five stations in a ring around London, to detect any aircraft approaching. These stations were called Chain Home.

The main base for the stations was a large house called Bawdsey Manor. There Robert Watson-Watt, his wife, and all of his assistants lived and worked, like a large family, intent upon a single goal: to defend England from enemy aircraft.

The need was so urgent that Robert and his assistants did not even take the time to create new equipment for the stations; instead they reused the parts they had already used in their tests, working to get the Chain Home stations up and running as quickly as possible. By September of 1936, they were ready for their first test. A whole group of British bombers would fly toward the coast of England, and Robert's stations would try to detect them in time for fighter pilots to intercept them.

The test was a disaster. None of the five stations received any reflected radio signals until the planes were already flying overhead! Too late! The officials from the government who were watching the test shook their heads in dismay.

But even as the planes were roaring away, Robert had already identified the problem. The transmitters that were sending out the radio pulses were not strong enough. Over the next few days, they repeated the test with more power to the transmitters, and they were able to detect the planes.

A final problem remained: once enemy airplanes were detected, the news needed to be given to the Air Force in time for them to send out their own fighter pilots. Robert solved this by setting up operation rooms, where all the information from Chain Home was sent and given to men whose job was to alert the British fighter pilots and tell them exactly where to go once their planes were in the air.

By 1937 the successful work of Chain Home inspired the British government to order the construction of many more radio detection stations all along the coast of England, to be called Chain Low. Work went on at a great pace, and by 1939 there were nineteen stations along the east coast and six more on the south, protecting the land from the far northern reaches of Scotland down to the English Channel. Each station had a huge steel tower, more than 250 feet tall, with the radio antenna perched on top. It could detect an aircraft 150 miles away.

The British and Robert Watson-Watt had always called this system "Radio Detection," but it had another name as well: RADAR, from the words RAdio Detection And Ranging. All over the world, other scientists and engineers were also working on radio detection, and the name RADAR actually came from America. But it was Robert Watson-Watt whose thunderstorm detection system began the whole idea, and it was he who believed firmly that radar would provide the key to protecting an entire nation. He found a practical way to make radar work, and his success with Chain Home inspired his government to quickly build a radar system.

And it is well that they did. By 1939 Chain Home and Chain Low were in place, their steel towers guarding the coasts and cities of England. And by 1939 England was at war with Adolf Hitler's Germany. His bombers were coming; their menace would soon fill the skies, but England was ready.

When we think about heroes, we do not usually picture a scientist working in his laboratory. We imagine a soldier fighting on a smoke-filled battlefield, or a fighter pilot aiming his plane straight toward an onrushing enemy. And we're right, of course; those men are heroes. But the scientist is a hero too. Without Robert Watson-Watt and his radar system, England would have fallen. Instead, England stood alone in Europe before the Nazis' conquering army. In the next story, you will hear how it happened.

Chapter 20

The Second World War

Are you wondering how it came to be that England was left standing alone to face the might of Nazi Germany? Let me tell you how it happened.

After their nation was swallowed up by depression and poverty in the 1920s, the German people had come to welcome Adolf Hitler as their leader. He promised that he would restore Germany to all of its former greatness and shake off the gloom and poverty that overshadowed their nation. By 1935 Hitler had gotten rid of any rivals to his power, and he had become the dictator of Germany, which means he was an absolute ruler whom no one could oppose. He did not call himself "dictator," of course. He deemed himself the "Fuhrer," or leader, of Germany and declared that the Germans were the rightful rulers of all of central Europe and must regain the lands that had once been theirs. He also told the Germans that they were a superior people, better than all others. The Nazis began to oppress anyone who was not a German, especially people who were Jews. There were many Jews in Germany in those years; the Nazis made them suffer, first by stealing or destroying their homes and shops, and later by doing much worse.

Hitler was not the only dictator to emerge from the sad years of the Great Depression. In Italy, a man named Benito Mussolini had seized power and named himself the absolute ruler. In Russia,

Joseph Stalin had begun to kill all who opposed him. In Japan, the emperor Hirohito and his army invaded nearby China, determined to seize the coal and iron with which China abounded and Japan lacked. Like Hitler and the Germans, the Japanese believed themselves to be a superior race of people, and they looked down with scorn upon the Chinese. Around the world, other nations watched in dismay as Germany, Japan, and Italy began to flex their muscles and threaten neighboring nations.

Italy invaded the nation of Ethiopia in Africa and then the tiny country of Albania in Europe. Japan pressed farther into China and sent its army into Russia as well. And then, in 1938, Germany marched into nearby Austria and calmly announced that it was taking over. After all, Hitler said, the Austrian homeland had always been a part of Germany in the past; he was just taking it back under his wing. The fact that the Austrians did not want to be a part of Germany mattered to Hitler not one bit, especially when the other nations of Europe did nothing to stop him. Encouraged, Hitler demanded that a large portion of Czechoslovakia be given to him as well. The Czechoslovakian leaders absolutely refused, but the leaders of France and Britain agreed to give some of the land to Hitler, if he would then promise to make no further demands. Helplessly, the Czech people watched as Nazis took over not just part but all of their nation. By 1939 there was no Czechoslovakia left; it had all become Germany.

Now, ignoring his promise, Hitler turned his eyes toward Poland, which had only just regained its independence from Russia a few years before. Greatly alarmed, France and Great Britain made a treaty with Poland, promising that they would help if it were threatened.

The treaty did not stop Hitler. On September 1st of 1939, his Nazi army invaded Poland, clearly intending to conquer it. And so, on September 3rd, France and Great Britain declared war on Germany.

Over in Asia, China and Japan were already battling each

other. War had begun, and it was spreading.

At first though, in Europe, nothing happened. Although war had been declared, no bullets flew and no bombs exploded. In England, the newspapers began calling it "the phony war," because nobody was fighting.

But Hitler was just biding his time. In 1940 he began to move, and his plans became frighteningly clear: he intended to conquer all of Europe. In April he invaded Norway and Denmark, and they surrendered to him. In May his armies swarmed over Belgium and the Netherlands; both were conquered in just a few weeks. The Nazis swept into France, forcing the British army there to scramble back across the English Channel. By June France was forced to surrender, and the French people watched Hitler himself parade down the broad avenues of Paris.

All of Europe lay at Hitler's feet. When France surrendered, only England remained to fight against him. Hitler was sure that the British would refuse such a battle and agree to a treaty with him. Then he could turn all of his attention to Russia, which he also intended to conquer. Some in Britain wanted to submit to Hitler's demands for a treaty; they feared that if they did not, they would be destroyed. But most of the British leaders and England's Prime Minister, Winston Churchill, refused to consider making peace with so evil a man as Hitler, even though they knew it meant a long and bitter war. Alone on their island, the British faced what seemed to be an unstoppable foe. Winston Churchill tried to prepare his people for what was to come: "The Battle of France is over," he said. "I expect that the Battle of Britain is about to begin." //

Indeed it was. Since Great Britain is an island, Hitler knew that in order to invade he would have to convey his soldiers onto the British coastline with boats. But boats would be an easy target for bomber airplanes; the British Royal Air Force had plenty of those, and they were ready to use them. So Hitler ordered an air campaign against Great Britain: he commanded his Air Force, the Luftwaffe, to destroy the Royal Air Force by bombing their airports and aircraft factories. Then, when the Air Force was gone, Hitler's army would invade England all at once, using many boats. When England fell, all of Europe would be his.

In August of 1940 Luftwaffe bombers began attacking England, aiming for the airfields and factories. But always the Royal Air Force was there to meet them. The German airplanes could never surprise their foes; the British fighters seemed to know their every move. And, of course, you know why. The huge steel radar towers lined the coastlines, and inside the operations rooms of Chain Home and Chain Low, the British radar operators could see the Luftwaffe coming. They sent the directions to the airfields, and the heroic British pilots raced to their airplanes and swarmed into the skies to meet the enemy.

Again and again the Luftwaffe attacked, and again and again they were driven back. But the costs were high on both sides, with many planes shot down and many pilots dead. The British decided to carry the battle away from their island; they began sending bombers over the city of Berlin in Germany.

Hitler was furious. How dare they attack his own city? He sent the Luftwaffe back to Britain with new orders. No longer would they limit themselves to airports and factories. Now Hitler wanted them to bomb the cities and towns of England. He wanted to destroy the fighting spirit of the British people.

Beginning on the night of September 7, 1940, German airplanes bombed the city of London and the surrounding towns for 76 nights in a row. More than a million houses and shops were destroyed, and thousands of people died. Again and again the radar operators gave warning and people raced for shelter in underground subways or in cellars in their backyards, and the British pilots rose into the skies to fight. The spirit of the people was not destroyed. They formed a Home Guard of citizens who were too old or too young to be regular soldiers, who swore to fight if the Nazis invaded their nation. They organized a volunteer

Fire Service to battle the flames that the bombs left behind. They had groups working continually at repair and clean-up.

They looked for inspiration to the Prime Minister, Winston Churchill, who spoke often over the radio, trying to encourage them. "We shall fight on the seas and oceans," he told them. "We shall fight with growing confidence and growing strength in the air, we shall defend our island, whatever the cost may be, we shall fight on the beaches, we shall fight on the landing grounds, we shall fight in the fields and in the streets, we shall fight in the hills; we shall never surrender!"

He praised the heroic efforts of the Air Force pilots, telling them, "Never in the field of human conflict was so much owed by so many to so few."

The people were suffering and many were dying, but Churchill urged them to stay strong and do what they could for each other and for their nation. "Let us therefore brace ourselves to our duties," he said, "so that if the British Empire last for a thousand years, men will still say, 'This was their finest hour!'"

Finally, on September 15th, two huge groups of Luftwaffe bombers were defeated and driven away by the Royal Air Force. After that, Hitler seemed to give up. He declared that the invasion of Britain would have to be postponed, perhaps until 1941. But the invasion never happened. Hitler turned his attention to Russia, and the bombing of Britain ended. By failing to conquer the British, Hitler and his Nazis suffered their first major defeat.

Meanwhile, over in Asia, the war between China and Japan had been fought to a standstill with neither side winning. Japan decided to change its plans. They wanted more land, or more precisely, they wanted more resources: oil, coal, wood. Their little island did not supply them with much of any of this, and they had been forced to buy most of it from other countries, especially the United States. If they could not conquer China and take its resources, they would have to look elsewhere. After signing a treaty with Germany and Russia, promising to fight with neither of them, the Japanese began to expand their empire by invading and seizing different parts of Indonesia.

Seeing this, though, the United States was angry and alarmed, and declared that it would sell no more oil to Japan, not at any price.

When they received that message, the Japanese made a further fateful decision: they would continue to press forward and try to seize all of the European colonies in Asia for themselves, since most of Europe was so distracted by Hitler. And, to prevent the United States from interfering with this plan, on December 7, 1941, they attacked the American islands of Hawaii, where most of the American Navy ships were docked at Pearl Harbor.

The United States immediately declared war on Japan. Germany responded by declaring war on the United States.

Now it was truly a World War. On one side, Nazi Germany, Japan, and Italy, along with all of their allies, became known as the Axis Powers. They faced the Allied Powers, whose main leaders were Great Britain, the United States, and Russia. As 1941 drew to a close, almost every nation on earth had been drawn into the mighty storm of World War II.

Chapter 21

The Underground

Have you ever played tug-of-war? Two groups of friends each pull on the end of a long rope and see which side can tug the other across a line drawn in the dirt. It is especially fun if the two groups are equal in size, so that it is not at all certain who will win. The rope is pulled backwards and forwards, until finally one side gives a mighty tug and the other side falls, laughing, across the line.

It would not be quite so amusing, though, if one of the groups was made up of your older brother and all of his tall friends, and the other, your little five-year-old sister and her playmates. The little girls might pull and tug with all their might, but no matter what they do, the big boys will surely win.

In Europe, during World War II, there was a tug-of-war that seemed just as lopsided as the little girls pulling against the big boys. But it was not a game; it was the deadly serious fight of the Underground Resistance against the Nazis.

Of course, the game of tug-of-war is all about resistance; each group digs in its heels and tries its best to resist the pulling of their opponents on the other end of the rope. In much the same way, all over Europe during the war, little bands of people did whatever they could to resist the Nazis' pull upon their nations. Hitler and his army had overthrown almost all the nations of Europe by 1941 and replaced those governments with their own.

This is called "occupation," when one victorious nation takes complete control of another. In the occupied nations of Europe, Hitler insisted that the people do as he commanded or suffer grave punishment. So during the day and out in the open, the people submitted themselves to his demands and tried to go about their daily lives. But during the dark of night and in shadowy hidden corners, they did whatever they could to resist him. But they had to keep their actions secret or risk imprisonment and death, and so the little groups of resistance fighters came to be called the Underground.

Underground armies organized themselves in all of the occupied countries, in Poland and Norway, in France and Belgium, Czechoslovakia and the Netherlands. They were armies not of soldiers, for the most part, but of ordinary people. Housewives, bakers, farmers, and schoolteachers, who outwardly seemed to be meekly obeying the Nazis, were instead risking their lives every day in secret battles fought not with bullets but with their wits and their courage.

One of the most important battles that the Underground fought was their efforts to save the Jewish people. As you learned in the previous story, Hitler hated anyone who wasn't German, and especially he hated the Jews. After he had conquered Europe, he began to arrest the Jews wherever he could find them and send them off to dreadful prison camps, where, secretly, he had them killed. It was a terrible evil.

The people who lived in the occupied nations realized that their Jewish neighbors were disappearing. In Poland several Underground leaders formed a special group called "The Council to Aid Jews," to provide whatever help they could. They provided false identity papers to Jews so that the Nazis would not know that they were Jewish. They gave the Jews who had gone into hiding food and medicine, and helped them sneak out of Poland. One Polish lady named Irena Sandler helped 2,500 Jewish children escape the Nazis by giving them false non-Jewish birth certificates and sheltering them in houses all over Poland.

One brave Polish man, Witold Pilecki, realized that something terrible must be happening to the Jews who were arrested by the Nazis. In order to find out, and to make it known to the rest of the world, he pretended to be a Jew and allowed himself to be arrested and shipped off with many other Jews to one of the prison camps. There he saw for himself that the Jews were being killed. He was able to smuggle secret reports out of the camp to other Underground workers, and they in turn were able to show the Allies that Hitler's evil was even greater than anyone had expected. After finding out all that he could, he managed to escape from the camp.

Of course, the Nazis realized that the Polish people were aiding the Jews, and they made it a crime punishable by death for any Pole to help a Jew. But that did not stop them; by the war's end, more than 50,000 Jewish people had been saved by the Underground resistance in Poland. More than one million Poles helped Jewish people in some way. And all over Europe, others aided the Jews in the same sorts of ways, hiding them in barns or attics, disguising them as long-lost cousins, or smuggling them out of the country in boats or cars. In Denmark, when Hitler ordered all Danish Jews arrested in 1943, almost every Jew in the country was whisked away to safety by the Danish people, in large fishing boats or in trains that Danish Underground workers had stolen from the Germans and disguised as ordinary freight cars filled with vegetables and grain.

The Underground helped others, too. Often, if an Allied fighter pilot was forced to crash land his plane in occupied lands, he would be taken prisoner at once by the Nazis. But if an Underground worker could get to him first, they would hide him, perhaps at a nearby farm, bring a doctor to him if he were injured, and then work on smuggling him back to the Allied armies. Sometimes Underground fighters even attacked prison camps to set the prisoners free.

In addition to saving Jews and Allied soldiers, Underground workers fought many other kinds of battles against the Nazis. For instance, the Underground performed a great deal of sabotage. Have you ever heard that word before? It means to deliberately weaken or destroy something that your enemy needs to use. The Nazis often forced the people in occupied nations to work in their factories, building guns or making bullets. But the people would do the work slowly or badly so that the guns wouldn't fire properly. Underground fighters also sabotaged roads and bridges that the Nazis were using, usually by blowing them up. They would cut telephone wires so the Nazis had trouble communicating; they would derail trains by removing sections of track, and empty water towers and destroy food storage centers so that the Nazi army ran short of supplies. They would creep out in the dark of night, in deepest secrecy, doing whatever they could to slow the Nazis down. Do you see why it was called Resistance? Even though the Nazis were big and powerful, the people in the Underground were pulling against them with all of their might.

Other groups of Underground fighters worked at helping the Allied armies, usually by providing them with news about what the Nazis were doing. This kind of spying was especially dangerous, because anyone caught trying to deliver a message to the Allies would be killed at once. Nevertheless, Underground spies were always watching. If they saw the Nazis bringing more soldiers into a certain area, they would find a way to get that information to the Allies, sometimes using codes in radio broadcasts or secret messages hid in unexpected places like inside the tires of a truck or in a pickle barrel with a false bottom. Thousands of written messages and radio broadcasts reached the Allies from Underground spies.

The Allies were helping the Underground, too. They realized that these secret fighters were just as determined as they to defeat Hitler. In England, Winston Churchill created a group of people whose only job was to help the Underground fighters in

Europe. This group was called the SOE, the "Special Operations Executive"; it was given such a strange name so if the Nazis heard of it, they would not know what it was. The SOE delivered small radios to help the resistance fighters in the occupied nations communicate with each other. It also sent spies, called "agents," throughout Europe to help the different Undergrounds accomplish their goals. SOE agents who were expert in explosives helped Underground fighters blow up bridges and railroad tracks. Agents who could speak flawlessly in German sneaked into occupied Paris and helped the Resistance there to spy on the Nazis. All over Europe the SOE battled Hitler by strengthening the Underground.

And so, by 1943, the Nazis were no longer moving forward. Hitler's stubborn Allied foes had stopped them. Unfortunately, they weren't moving backward either. Most of Europe was still occupied, and Hitler was busy making plans for more conquest. He would have to be driven back into Germany; he would have to be utterly conquered or his evil would never stop. The Allies and their friends in the Underground would have to try something new. It was time for Operation Overlord; it was time for D-Day.

Chapter 22

The Day of Days

In 1943 the tentacles of Nazi power were tightly wrapped around most of Europe, and Germany seemed unstoppable. The German factories, many of them filled with slave workers from conquered nations, seemed to be producing plenty of supplies. The German people had more than enough to eat, even while German submarines were sinking every supply ship they could find out in the Atlantic Ocean, so that the people of Britain often went hungry. German engineers were busily building concrete fortresses all along the borders of Germany and the coastline of France. It was obvious to the Allied leaders that, unless they did something drastic, Hitler's hold on Europe would never be broken. The Allies knew that they were going to have to invade.

Joseph Stalin, the dictator of Russia, had wanted the Allies to invade Europe since 1942. Hitler had moved his armies into Russia in 1941, and Stalin desperately wanted to be rid of him. Surely the best way to distract Hitler from his plan to conquer Russia would be to present the huge new threat of an invading Allied army. Stalin had been pressing this idea on Winston Churchill and the American president, Franklin Roosevelt.

But Roosevelt refused. The Americans were not ready; their navy was out fighting the Japanese in the Pacific Ocean; they were still forming their army; and they needed to build many more boats and ships in order to carry an army across the English

Channel from Britain to Nazi-occupied France. Both Roosevelt and Churchill knew, though, that attacking Hitler in France was the only possible way to defeat him. We will go when we are prepared, they told Stalin. Then Roosevelt appointed an army general named Dwight D. Eisenhower to come up with a plan for the invasion of Europe. The date of May 1944, was chosen. Stalin agreed that he would mount a battle against Hitler in Russia on that same date, and together, the Allies would try to overwhelm the Nazis.

The invasion was given the code name Operation Overlord. With General Eisenhower commanding, a huge army of American, British, and Canadian soldiers would land in Normandy in northern France. If you look at a map of Europe and find the islands of Great Britain, you will see Normandy just to the south, across the narrow waters of the English Channel. If you study it more closely, you will see a peninsula jutting up from the Normandy coast like a jaunty thumb. This is the Cotentin Peninsula. Along its left-hand side there are several long beaches, and it was five of these beaches that were the Allies' target. They were lonely places with no ports or towns, and the Allies hoped that the Germans would not expect an invasion there. They were given code names: the British would aim for Gold and Sword beaches, the Canadians for Juno beach, and the Americans for Utah and Omaha beaches. After they had secured the beaches, the Allies planned to march forward through France, driving the Germans back until France was free. Then they would invade Germany itself.

Hitler knew that the Allies were planning an invasion, and he was prepared. All of the beaches that faced the English Channel were littered with millions of mines—little bombs buried in the sand, set to explode if stepped on by a soldier. The coastline bristled with concrete fortresses, filled with German soldiers and topped with huge cannons. Hitler called this his Atlantic Wall, and he was convinced that it would stop any invasion attempt. His general, Erwin Rommel, was not so sure. If the Allies attack, he told Hitler, I must push them back into the sea within a few days or I will never get them out of France. Hitler scoffed at that. They will never succeed, he said. The Wall will stop them.

The Allies continued their planning all through 1943. General Eisenhower put a British commander, Bernard Montgomery, in charge of the soldiers who would fight on the ground. He also made plans to attack from the air; after all, when Hitler had built his Atlantic Wall, he had neglected to put a roof on it. Dozens of planes would fly over Normandy just ahead of the boats and drop groups of paratroopers, which are soldiers who jump out of airplanes with parachutes. Eisenhower appointed one of his lieutenants, General J. C. H. Lee, to organize the thousands and thousands of ships and boats that would be needed to transport not just 160,000 soldiers, but also tanks and trucks and 600,000 tons of supplies. An army travels with a great deal of luggage!

In the spring of 1944, the plan for invasion was set in motion. Hundreds of bombers were sent over to France, dropping bombs on German airfields and airplanes, on roads and railroad tracks, and especially on bridges, so that the invasion area in Normandy was isolated from the rest of France. This would keep the Germans from easily sending in tanks and reinforcements. The Allies also tried to deceive the Germans by dropping bombs in areas far away from Normandy, so Hitler could not be sure from which direction the invasion would come. The Underground in France went to work, often risking their lives to spy on the Germans so they could let the Allies know exactly how the Germans were preparing to defend against the invasion. As the day of invasion drew close, the Underground sent out its secret soldiers, who cut telephone lines, destroyed gasoline stations, and derailed trains.

By the end of May, the Allies were ready. But all of Normandy was lashed by heavy rain and swirling winds, and the English Channel was swamped with dangerous, towering waves. General Eisenhower waited impatiently throughout the first days of June until the weathermen assured him that the storms were receding.

"Okay," he said, "we'll go." The invasion would begin on the next day, June 6, 1944. It was code-named D-Day.

General Eisenhower sent a message to each soldier in the Allied army. In it he said this:

> Soldiers, Sailors and Airman of the Allied Expeditionary Force! You are about to embark upon a great crusade, toward which we have striven these many months. The eyes of the world are upon you. The hopes and prayers of liberty-loving people everywhere march with you. In company with our brave Allies and brothers in arms, you will bring about the destruction of the German war machine, the elimination of Nazi tyranny over the oppressed peoples of Europe, and security for ourselves in a free world.
>
> I have full confidence in your courage, devotion to duty and skill in battle. We will accept nothing less than full victory! Good Luck! And let us all beseech the blessings of Almighty God upon this great and noble undertaking.

That night 822 planes rose up from England's airfields, each one carrying a small squad of paratroopers. Six thousand boats and ships left England's ports, loaded with the invading army and all of its supplies. It was the largest invading force in history.

The airborne troops were supposed to land first, parachuting in behind the German fortresses along the coast and attacking them from the rear. But things did not go exactly as planned. The heavy clouds forced the pilots to fly low and fast, and many of them got lost, scattering all over Normandy. When the Germans realized they were there and began firing their guns into the sky, the pilots shouted for the troopers to jump out at once. They ended up in isolated little bands, far from their planned landing sites and, most of the time, separated from their leaders and their fellow troopers. But this seeming disaster actually became an unplanned advantage for the Allies. The Germans heard reports of parachutes from every corner of Normandy; they thought the Allies had dropped thousands of troopers into battle. The German leaders began sending their soldiers here, there, and everywhere, wasting much time and effort to chase after troopers who did not actually exist. The Germans spread themselves so thin that the real troopers were able to easily slip through and join together again with their fellows. They began to attack the Germans like a force of ghosts, firing their guns and then slipping elusively away.

Meanwhile, the British, Canadian, and American soldiers were approaching the five beaches. Gold, Juno, and Sword beaches were only lightly defended, perhaps because so many Germans were out chasing phantom troopers or because the Germans simply did not expect the Allies to attack such isolated places. The British and Canadian soldiers overwhelmed the Germans and took the beaches, as did the American troops at Utah Beach. But at Omaha Beach, the Americans faced huge obstacles. The beach was wide, almost six miles long, and it was overlooked along its entire length by tall cliffs topped with German fortresses. Hundreds of the best German soldiers were firing their guns down at the Americans as they tried to wade ashore. Many died, and it began to look as if the invasion at Omaha Beach would fail. The soldiers knew that their only hope was to scale the cliffs. Gradually, in little groups held together only by extreme courage, the soldiers managed to find ways off the terrible beach and up the cliffs. From there, they could directly attack the Germans in their fortresses. Eventually, at great cost, they were able to beat the Germans back and take possession of the beach and the cliffs above.

General Omar Bradley, who was in charge of the soldiers at Omaha Beach, talked about it years later. "Even now it brings pain to recall what happened there on June 6, 1944. I have returned many times to honor the valiant men who died on that beach. They should never be forgotten. Nor should those who lived to carry that day by the slimmest of margins. Every man who set foot on Omaha Beach that day was a hero."

Now the Allies had a beachhead, a toehold on Nazi-occupied Europe. Throughout that day of days, the soldiers fought, pushing the Germans back away from the coastline, forcing them to abandon their concrete fortresses. By the end of the day, the Germans had begun to retreat across Normandy. They were still battling fiercely, and the war was far from over, but it was the beginning of the end. The German general Rommel had been correct; he did not manage to push the Allies back into the sea, and he never did get them out of France.

The cost of D-Day was great; four thousand soldiers lost their lives. But their sacrifice was not in vain. Now the Allies would take the battle directly to Hitler, and they would defeat him. For the next year, the Allies forced the Germans to retreat. By August of 1944, Paris was free from Nazi control. By September, Allied troops had reached the border of Germany. In December, Hitler sent his soldiers forward in a last desperate attempt to regain control, but it failed. Throughout the spring of 1945, the Germans were pushed back, and in March the Allies crossed the Rhine River and entered Germany itself. Finally, on May 7th, Germany surrendered. Hitler himself was dead, killed by his own hand.

In Italy, Hitler's ally Benito Mussolini was killed by his own people. In Japan, the United States ended the war by dropping two huge bombs and forcing the Japanese to surrender. By September 1945, the Allies were victorious, and World War II was over.

Chapter 23

A Useful Accident

On a warm September morning in 1928, a scientist named Alexander Fleming unlocked the door of his laboratory and prepared for another day of research. The room was terribly untidy: books and notes in uneven piles, unwashed beakers stacked in the sink, sketches and diagrams pinned haphazardly to the walls. Dr. Fleming surveyed this mess with a smile. He was refreshed and full of energy, since he had just returned from a two-week family vacation in the country, and what is more, he liked untidiness. He felt that messy rooms led to unexpected ideas, so he never threw anything away. "Just put that aside," he would always say. "It may come in useful."

Hanging up his coat and hat, he stepped over to his large work bench. There, on one end, was a stack of petri dishes: flat plates on which scientists grow bacteria. These particular dishes had been used by Dr. Fleming to grow a bacteria called staphylococci, a nasty germ that causes sore throats and other infections. Dr. Fleming had finished the experiment before he had left for his vacation, but he had not yet cleaned the petri dishes. He gathered some cleansing cloths and soap and then set about scrubbing the plates.

The door to the laboratory opened, and a friend walked in, a man named Merlin Pryce. He noticed the sink full of suds and the piles of dirty petri dishes and chuckled. "Doing my old job, are you?" he asked. Mr. Pryce had at one time been Dr. Fleming's assistant.

"Merlin," said Dr. Fleming, holding up one of the dishes, "look at this. This dish has been contaminated with some sort of mold, I think. And look. The mold has killed the bacteria."

Merlin stepped closer and peered at the dish that the doctor was holding. It was covered with bacteria along its edges; but in its center was a ring-shaped growth of fuzzy green mold, and all around the mold, the bacteria was completely gone.

"Strange," Merlin said agreeably. He was used to Dr. Fleming's interest in even the smallest matter.

"More than just strange, I think," Dr. Fleming said. "This is rather exciting!"

Alexander Fleming had been interested in germs for a long time. He had begun working with bacteria as a young medical student, especially the bacteria that cause infections in wounds. During the Great War, he had served in the medical units and had seen firsthand the terrible damage that infections wrought on wounded soldiers. He worked tirelessly throughout the war, specializing in the treatment of infection and saving the lives of many soldiers.

Even after the war ended, Dr. Fleming had devoted himself to research. He often worked until the early hours of the morning, went home to sleep a few hours, and then returned to his laboratory at 9:00 A.M., ready to continue. If he needed a blood sample for his work, he would usually take it from his own arm. If he needed to test a vaccine, he would test it on himself first.

In those years, between the end of the Great War and that September morning in 1928, Dr. Fleming was working on ways to slow or even stop the growth of germs. One day, during the winter of 1920, he had come to work with a cold. Not wanting to waste his own germs, he had placed a sample of the mucus from his nose in a petri dish of bacteria. The germs refused to grow anywhere near the mucus. Encouraged by this, he decided to try another body fluid, tears from his eyes, to see if it would also discourage the bacteria. To get a big enough sample, he squeezed the juice from a lemon directly into his eyes.

When the tears, too, prevented the bacteria from growing, Dr. Fleming knew he was on a useful trail. After gathering samples from and performing experiments with saliva, skin, internal organs, fingernails, and anything else he could think of, Dr. Fleming proved that many parts of the human body will naturally destroy bacteria. It was an important discovery, but his tests showed that the bacteria destroyed were usually harmless germs, not the dangerous ones that cause infection. As interesting as this work was, Dr. Fleming still wanted to find a way to kill the deadliest infections.

And so, eight years later, on that September morning, he stared down at the fuzzy ring in his petri dish with growing excitement. Whatever this mold was, it had not just prevented the bacteria from growing; it had actually killed the germs. He knew at once that this could be a finding of the utmost importance.

First, though, he must identify the mold. He had left the window open while he had been gone on vacation, and he surmised that a tiny spore of mold must have floated in and landed on the petri dish. But what was it? There are many different kinds of molds and fungi, and Dr. Fleming was not an expert in that field. He read through every book he could find about molds and determined that this particular one was from a family of molds called *penicillium*.

Dr. Fleming and his assistants began growing *penicillium* in large jars of beef broth set up on a long table in the hallway outside his laboratory. He called this concoction "mold juice," and, using it, he began to experiment on many different kinds of bacteria: the germs that cause fevers and pneumonia, strep throat and blood poisoning. The *penicillium* mold killed them all. Dr. Fleming knew now that he had discovered a wonder drug, a medicine that could cure many deadly infections. He also knew that he needed a better name for it than "mold juice," so he christened it "penicillin."

Before it could become a true medicine, penicillin needed more work. The *penicillium* mold was a living creature, and that made it difficult to store and to create in large quantities. The bacteria-killing part must be isolated and extracted from the mold, so that it could then be manufactured as a tablet or an injection that could be given to infected patients. This kind of work would have to be done by a different kind of scientist: a chemist, which is someone who studies the parts that make up things, and how to separate those parts from one another. Dr. Fleming was not a chemist, and so he knew that his role in the story of penicillin was over. He wrote papers and presented them to other scientists, explaining his discovery, and he sent samples of the *penicillium* mold to any scientist who asked for it. He insisted to anyone who would listen that penicillin could save the lives of millions of people if only it could be made widely available.

Finally, in the late 1930s, two chemists at Oxford University in England took up the challenge. Their names were Howard Florey, who had come from Australia, and Ernst Chain, a Jew who had fled from Adolf Hitler's Nazi Germany. They could see that the drums of war were beating loudly throughout Europe, and they knew that penicillin, if it could be purified into an actual medicine, could save the lives of multitudes of soldiers. They worked to find ways to grow the *penicillium* in bigger quantities, and they even found a faster-growing form of the mold on some melons from a local market. They decided to see if they could come up with a way to make it into a substance that could be injected into a sick or wounded person's body.

By 1940 they had found a way. On May 25th they performed their most important test. They injected eight mice with a deadly bacteria, and then four of them with penicillin. The untreated mice died quickly, but the four that had received the penicillin recovered completely, running about their cages in exuberant good health. The medicine worked. Now they tested it on patients, desperately ill with infections that would kill them. The penicillin saved their lives, and the scientists knew that they had found a way to benefit all mankind. They persuaded a large company in the United States to devote itself exclusively to manufacturing penicillin, and by D-Day in 1944, they had enough penicillin made and stockpiled to treat every single soldier in the war if needed. Throughout the war, the injections of penicillin cured terrible infections suffered both by thousands of soldiers and also many ordinary people.

After World War II was over, other companies began to manufacture the medicine as well and distribute it throughout the world. From 1940 right on through to this very day, penicillin has saved, and continues to save, millions of lives that would otherwise be lost to the deadly infections that can come with illness or injury.

What would have happened if Dr. Fleming had not noticed that dirty petri dish or had not realized what it might mean? Perhaps we should all be thankful that Alexander Fleming was happy to work in a messy laboratory and was curious and observant enough to take a second look at a fuzzy ring of mold.

Chapter 24

The Creation of Israel

Y ou may have noticed, as you have been reading about history, that many stories, no matter at which point you start to read them, have a beginning that is lost far back in the mists of time and an ending which is not yet come to pass. This is the case of the story of Israel, whose people have wandered the earth for two thousand years and whose nation has only existed since 1948. It is a story that still goes on today.

The modern nation of Israel sits upon the site of the ancient Jewish kingdoms of David and Solomon, the land where Joshua fought at Jericho and Jesus was born, and where Herod the Great built a mighty Temple for the worship of God. There, the city of Jerusalem crowns the hills above the Dead Sea, and the tomb of Abraham rests in a cave in Hebron.

When the majestic city of Rome spread its conquering robe over that region of the world, they renamed it Palaestina and so it came to be called Palestine, and the nation that was Israel disappeared from the earth. The Romans destroyed the Temple of Herod and ruled the region with a fist of iron. While some of the Jewish people stayed there in Palestine, many more spread all over the world, to Africa and to Greece and then Spain and then onward into the rest of Europe. But theirs was not an easy life; many people hated them and treated them harshly, making them live in separate, poorer parts of their cities, stealing their money or goods, and sometimes even taking their lives for no reason except that they were Jewish.

When the rule of Rome ended, Palestine came under the control of Arab caliphs and sultans, and Islam became the religion of that place. A large and very beautiful mosque, which is a place of worship for those who follow Islam, was built over the ruins of the Temple, and Jerusalem became a mostly Muslim city. Jews still lived there, at peace with their Arab neighbors, but only a minority in what had once been their great capital city.

By the nineteenth century, most Jews, about five million of them, lived in the eastern part of the Russian Empire, ruled by the tsar, who often treated them as if they were an enemy. Many Jewish people in Russia were not allowed to live in Russian towns and, so, were forced to create their own separate villages. They were not allowed to be doctors or lawyers, and Jewish boys were required to spend twenty-five years of their lives serving in the Russian army. In other countries in Europe, the Jewish people were not treated much better. As their lives grew more and more difficult, many Jews decided to immigrate to a new nation, the United States of America, in the hope of building lives free from persecution. In Palestine some Jews still lived their quiet lives, but only a very few of them. Other Jews looked at them thoughtfully, and slowly a murmur began to grow amongst the Jewish people: could we not consider re-making the nation of Israel? Could we not be an independent people again?

So, in 1878, a small group of Jewish people left their homes in Europe and America, and traveled to Palestine to establish a little Jewish village. They began to revive the ancient Hebrew language, which had been used by Jews two thousand years before, and to encourage others to join them. Many did. They formed collective farms, which means that they all lived and worked together. By 1909 they established the first entirely Hebrew-speaking city, along the coast of the Mediterranean Sea, which came to be called Tel Aviv. They began to publish a Hebrew newspaper and to organize a kind of government, even though they were not really a nation.

During the terrible years of the Great War, Palestine was under the control of the British empire. Many Jews supported the cause of Great Britain and fought in her armies. In gratitude, the British government made a declaration to the world: "We view with favour the establishment in Palestine of a national home for the Jewish people."

Now, you may be thinking, and rightly so, that for all of those years since the fall of Rome, Palestine had been home to Arab people, Muslims who considered Jerusalem and Palestine to be their own. Of course, they viewed the Jewish settlements and the British declaration with growing alarm. What would happen to them if Palestine became a Jewish nation? Would they have to leave? Would they be treated fairly? The British declaration went on to say that "nothing shall be done to prejudice the rights of the existing non-Jewish communities in Palestine," but the Arab people living there did not find that very reassuring.

Jewish people continued to come, some 40,000 of them between the years of 1919 and 1923. Most of them came from Russia, which was still in great turmoil due to the Revolution there. They called themselves *halutzim*: pioneers. They were experienced farmers, and they were used to creating their own villages, for that is what they had been forced to do in Russia. In some of the valleys and plains of Palestine, they drained marshes and plowed land, making green and fruitful farms where none had existed before.

By 1929, 82,000 more had come. They were fleeing the rise of the Nazis in Germany and the growing hatred for their people. They opened workshops and small markets, and built schools and hospitals.

By now the Arab people living in Palestine were feeling desperate and frightened and, most of all, angry. This was their land! It was true that the Jews had purchased the land they were using; they had not stolen it. But the Arabs could see no end to the flow of Jewish pioneers, and to them it looked as if Palestine would soon be wholly Jewish. They began to attack, with words and sometimes with weapons. The Jews, now worried themselves, began to set up a secret army to protect their villages.

The British tried to quiet the growing storm. They recommended an independent nation of Palestine be established, to be ruled by both Jews and Arabs. But both Jewish and Arab leaders rejected the idea, and anger on both sides continued to grow. In order to placate the Arabs, the British then issued a law forbidding the Jews to buy any more land in Palestine.

And then came World War II.

Since the Nazis were determined to kill all of them, the Jews viewed Hitler and his Axis allies as their most bitter enemy. More than one million Jewish young men joined in the fight against him, serving in the British, Russian, and American armies. And then, at the end of the war, the world became aware of the horrible destruction that the Nazis had brought down upon the Jews who had remained in Europe. The large communities of Jewish people who had lived in Poland and Germany were gone forever; most of them had been killed. The remnant of Jews left in Europe were refugees: they had no homes, no communities, and no roots left. When asked, 97 percent of them insisted that they wanted to immigrate to Palestine.

After the war, the nations of the world had joined together to create a group called the United Nations, where leaders could meet and discuss problems that affected the world at large. In 1947 the British government brought the problem of Palestine to the United Nations. What could be done? The Jews needed a home, but the Arabs did not want them there. There was a great deal of debate; perhaps a Jewish nation could be created somewhere else. There was lots of empty space in Canada. How about there? Or in South America? But the Jews insisted that Palestine was their natural home. David had been king there. Abraham and Sarah were buried there. The Temple was there, its foundation's stones still visible underneath the Arab mosque in Jerusalem.

At last, the United Nations declared that Palestine should be divided in two, with separate states, one Arab and one Jewish, and the city of Jerusalem belonging to neither, but under the control of a United Nations committee. This idea pleased no one, and, by this time, the Arabs in Palestine and all of the neighboring Arab nations were insisting that they would greet any attempt to create a Jewish nation with all-out war. Fighting between the Arabs and Jews within Palestine began to grow, especially as the British began withdrawing all of their people in 1948.

As soon as the last of the British army forces left, on May 14, 1948, the Jewish people declared the establishment of the nation of Israel, in accordance with the United Nations' declaration. There were 650,000 Jews living in Palestine on that day, and more than one million Arab people.

The neighboring Arab nations—Egypt, Jordan, Syria, Lebanon, and Iraq—immediately declared war on the new nation and invaded it at once, determined to get rid of it before it had any chance to establish itself. But the new and tiny nation of Israel had an efficient and highly organized army. Remember the secret army? It was no secret now; it was filled with tough young men who had fought all through World War II and knew a great deal about battles and weapons. It was led by generals who had experienced years of war. And all of its soldiers and leaders were grim and determined, because they knew they were fighting for their very existence as a people.

At first, the Arabs were successful. Their soldiers took control of the city of Jerusalem and large portions of the land that the Jews had been given by the United Nations. But the Israeli army, centered in the city of Tel Aviv, fought back, seizing the land along the Mediterranean Sea and pressing inland until they had taken back the town of Nazareth. They continued to probe southward toward Egypt as well. For the Arabs, the war became more grueling. Their supply lines were very long, and easily cut, and so they had difficulties bringing in food and water and ammunition for their soldiers.

In June and then again in July, the Israelis and the Arabs agreed to short truces, so that both sides could rest and gather supplies and strength. After the second truce, the Israelis focused all of their efforts on attacking south, in Egypt. They won several victories, and in January of 1949, the Egyptians asked for an armistice, which, you will remember, is an agreement between two enemies to cease fighting.

Throughout 1949 the new nation of Israel signed armistices with all five of the Arab nations who had invaded. But Arabs still remained in control of several sections of Palestine. The Syrians occupied a small strip of territory along the Sea of Galilee; the Egyptians controlled a little strand along the Mediterranean called the Gaza Strip; and the nation of Jordan held sway over the eastern half of the city of Jerusalem. This situation was bitter indeed for the Israelis, but it did not stop hundreds of thousands of Jews from streaming into Israel.

In three years, from 1948 to 1951, the population of Israel doubled. Most of these new Israelis were either Jews who had survived Hitler's attempts to kill them in Europe or Jews who were fleeing Arab lands where they no longer felt welcome. By 1958 two million Jews were living in Israel. It was a hard time for the new little country, since many of these immigrants had left everything behind to come to Israel, and so were very poor. But Jews living elsewhere, especially in the United States, sent money to help, and gradually Israel grew more prosperous.

Now the Israelis felt they must do something about the Arab-controlled portions of their land. On June 5, 1967, they struck swiftly. The Israeli air force destroyed the air forces of Egypt, Syria, and Jordan, and then, with their army, Israel attacked those three nations. By June 11th the Arab armies had been defeated and Israel had gained control of the Gaza Strip, the Syrian territory in

Galilee, and, perhaps most importantly, East Jerusalem. Everyone who was living in those areas was immediately given citizenship in the nation of Israel. Jews around the world rejoiced.

But, of course, Arabs did not, for to the Arab nations nothing about the creation of Israel was a cause for joy. In their minds, Palestine was still Arab land. So while some view the nation of Israel as a great victory, to others it is a sorrow and a defeat. Do you remember all those armistices that Israel signed with its Arab neighbors in 1949? None of them were ever made into formal peace treaties. War between Israel and the Arabs could resume at any time. That is why the story is still going on to this very day.

Chapter 25

The Dead Sea Scrolls

I hope you remember our story about the building of the Suez Canal, with the ships gliding through the windblown sand, for I would like to ask you to picture that desert place again. Can you see the golden dunes and the dusty brown outcroppings of weathered rock? Try to keep that picture in your mind as I tell you this next tale.

In the early spring of 1947, just after World War II had ended, a young shepherd boy named Jum'a was roaming through the barren hills above the northwest shore of the Dead Sea, searching for a lost goat. He made his away along a faint trail, absently tossing pebbles and eyeing the crumbling limestone cliffs, looking for some sign of movement that might indicate his lost quarry, so he could gather it up and go home to his family's large black tent. Gradually, he realized that the dark shadows that he was seeing further up the cliff sides were not actually shadows at all, but were instead holes in the rocks. Caves! he thought excitedly. Then, as any boy would have done, he scrambled a bit closer to one of the openings and threw in a stone to see how deep it might be.

To his surprise, he heard, not the clatter of his stone striking the rocky bottom of the cave, but rather the sharp crack of shattering pottery. Something other than rock and air was down in that cave! As he climbed closer, he realized that the opening was big enough for a boy to fit through, an interesting discovery indeed. Regretfully, he turned away. There was no time today to explore; he must find the lost goat and return to his family, who would be expecting him by sundown. He resolved to come back as soon as he could.

Some days later the bright spring sun found Jum'a and his cousin Muhammed picking their way up the hillside toward the cave. After hearing Jum'a's story, Muhammed had been eager to come along and see what they could find.

The opening to the cave was difficult to reach, and its edges were crumbling and unstable. Perhaps it will not surprise any of my readers to learn that, when they finally reached the cave, Muhammed lost his footing and fell right down into the cave's dark mouth! He picked himself up and looked back up to the cave's opening, where Juma's concerned face was silhouetted against the sun's brilliant light. Muhammed assured his cousin that he was not injured, and then he began feeling around in the dim light. He was cautious, for he was not sure what other desert dwellers, some with fangs or claws, might also have discovered this cool, sheltered hole in the rock. He could faintly see some large earthen jars, one of which had been broken by Jum'a's stone. There, amongst the fragments, he could see several large, oblong objects. He gathered three of them up, and then, clumsily, he clambered up the uneven wall of the cave far enough to reach Juma's outstretched hand.

Out in the sunlight, the two boys examined their find. The objects were wrapped in linen. Underneath the cloth they were made of parchment, tightly rolled: they were scrolls. Muhammed and Jum'a decided to take them back to their families.

The boys belonged to a tribe of wandering shepherds called Bedouins, who lived in tents and herded goats and sheep for their living. The elders in the tribe studied the scrolls carefully, but no one could recall ever having seen anything like them before. They were not sure what to do with them: keep them, use them as fuel for their fires, throw them away? Until they could decide, they hung them carefully from the center pole of one of the tents. Whenever the tribe received a visitor, one of the elders would bring out the scrolls and display them, asking, "Have you ever seen this before? Do you know what these are?"

Eventually, the Bedouins decided to take the scrolls into the little town of Bethlehem, which was nearby. Yes, the same little Bethlehem where Jesus was born nearly two thousand years earlier. A shopkeeper there was rumored to know something about old things. This man, though, after looking at the scrolls, returned them to the tribe, shaking his head. "They are worth nothing," he said. "Perhaps they were stolen from a synagogue." A synagogue is a place where Jews gather to worship, and most synagogues have scrolls with the Hebrew scriptures written on them.

The Bedouins thanked him politely, but they were not convinced that he was right. So they took the scrolls to another market, and then to another, and eventually they found an antiques dealer who was willing to buy them, if the boys would show him the site where they had been found. The tribe agreed and left the scrolls in the hands of a scholar who lived nearby until the sale could be arranged to the satisfaction of all concerned.

Now this scholar was a Syrian, and so he sent a message to a Syrian Christian monastery nearby, asking if someone there would come and look at these old scrolls. I'm sure you remember that a monastery is a place where men called monks live and work, dedicating their lives to God. The most senior monk at this monastery was a man named Mar Samuel, and he came to examine the scrolls. They were from the Bible, he saw, containing the book of Isaiah. He realized that they were old indeed, and he sent word at once to the Bedouins that he was also very interested in purchasing their find.

Meanwhile, three more scrolls appeared, offered for sale in the market. Some in the Bedouin tribe must have returned to the cave and gathered up what was left to be found there. Two professors from the Hebrew University in Jerusalem,

Eleazar Sukenik and Benjamin Mazar, bought them. They were archaeologists, who dug up and studied the relics of the past. They knew that these scrolls were something very unique. Here is what Professor Sukenik said about that day: "My hands shook as I started to unwrap one of them. I read a few of the sentences. It was written in beautiful biblical Hebrew. I looked and I looked, and I suddenly had the feeling that I was privileged by destiny to gaze upon a Hebrew scroll which had not been read for more than 2,000 years." Soon, the two professors learned of the other scrolls that Mar Samuel had at the monastery.

Now an American scholar named Dr. John Trever heard about all of this. He studied the scrolls, comparing them to the oldest manuscript of the Bible that then existed. The text differed hardly at all. The scrolls were definitely copies of the Bible, but they were far older that any previously known, almost one thousand years older! How faithfully the words of the Bible had been transcribed over the centuries!

By now it was 1948, and as we saw in the previous story, this region of the world was filled with fighting and war. None of the scholars had been able to persuade the Bedouin tribe to reveal the location of the cave where the scrolls had been found, and they were worried that, if there were any more scrolls, they might be damaged or destroyed. Then, in January of 1949, a Belgian military officer, who was assigned to the area because of the fighting, managed to locate the cave. He informed the scholars, and they began at once to explore further. Very soon after that, they discovered that there were other caves in the crumbling limestone cliffs.

The caves were near an ancient ruined town called Khirbet Qumran, and so the site became known as the Qumran Caves. The scrolls themselves are called the Dead Sea Scrolls, because the cliffs overlook the sparkling blue waters of that desert lake.

By 1952 eight more caves had been discovered, and many more scrolls. All told, the Dead Sea Scrolls contain at least fragments of every book in the Bible's Old Testament, except for the story of Esther.

Who could have done all this copying and collecting?

Long ago, a group of Jewish scribes lived in the town of Qumran. Many of you might know that a scribe is a person who copies manuscripts; he spends his days with pen and ink, painstakingly copying until the letters must start swimming before his eyes! This particular group of scribes was called the Essenes, and they lived communally, which means that they all lived together and shared everything they owned. They were very peaceful people, ancient historians tell us. They never carried weapons, always spoke softly, and refused to own slaves. Each morning, each one would bathe in cold water and then join the rest of the group for prayer and a meal in a large room all together. For three hundred years, from about two centuries before the birth of Jesus until about one hundred years after it, they did their work, living very simply and separating themselves from other people. The scrolls must have been their library. They copied the words from scrolls that were even older and have now been lost.

Now I imagine some of my readers are asking, "Why did they decide to hide their scrolls in the caves of Qumran?" Well, I will tell you, but it is not a happy story.

Sixty-eight years after Jesus was born, the Jews who lived in that part of the world decided to rebel against their masters. Do you remember who was master of the world during that time in history? If you are thinking Rome, then you are correct! And if you have read anything at all about the Romans, perhaps you can guess that the Emperor of Rome did not take kindly to any people's rebellion against his power. He sent legions of Roman soldiers to destroy the Jewish rebels and burn their towns and cities so that they would never rise against him again.

The Essenes must have known that they were in danger. And so, they hid their precious scrolls in large jars and secreted them in the caves all around their town.

It was well that they did so; for the Romans destroyed Khirbet Qumran, and no one ever returned to retrieve the scrolls until Muhammed fell into the cave on that day in 1948.

You yourself may look at these ancient words any time you please, because scholars have put careful pictures of the scrolls on the Internet, where all may view them. And if you would like to look at them with your own eyes, you can travel to Jerusalem, where, in a specially-lighted cave-shaped museum, the scrolls wait even today.

Chapter 26

Kon Tiki

L ate one night, in the summer of 1937, as tropical breezes caressed the palm trees outside an island hut, a man named Thor Heyerdahl tossed restlessly in his hammock. His wife slept peacefully at his side, but Dr. Heyerdahl could not rest. As a scientist, he had been studying the culture of the native people who had lived for hundreds of years on this island and on others like it here in the South Seas. The people had been pleased to share their lives with this interested stranger and had cooked food for him, performed their ancient dances for him, and most of all, displayed their art for him. It was the artwork that kept him wakeful now. The natives had shown him, in particular, many stone statues of squat, powerful-looking men with fierce faces, their hands curved in front of their bellies as if they were ready to jump up and fight. The statues captivated Dr. Heyerdahl, because he knew at once that he had seen others like them, but not here. He had gazed upon these same kinds of statues thousands of miles away, when he had been studying the people of Peru, the ancient Inca Indians, in South America.

How could such similar statues have been created by completely different people separated by vast miles of ocean? As he stared up at the hut's dark ceiling, Dr. Heyerdahl had an arresting thought: perhaps they were *not* different people. What if the people who carved the island statues were the same people who had made the statues in Peru?

At first it did not seem possible. After all, as you yourself may see if you look at your globe, Peru is almost half a world away from the South Sea Islands, with nothing between them but blue water. And, furthermore, most of the other scientists who studied the people of the South Seas believed that they came from Asia. No one had ever suggested that they came from anywhere else.

Filled with excitement at his new idea, Dr. Heyerdahl returned to his home in Norway. He wrote a paper explaining his thoughts and waited to see what his fellow scientists would say. They were not encouraging. It is too far, they said. The Peruvian people could never have sailed across all of that ocean. The only boats they possessed were rafts made from logs, and a person could never cross 4,000 miles of ocean on a log raft!

Dr. Heyerdahl was not discouraged by these comments, but he knew that in order to gain acceptance for his idea, he would have to prove that it was possible. He decided to build a raft, using only the types of materials that the ancient people of Peru would have had available. Then he would set sail from the coast of Peru and see how far west he could get. He believed very strongly that he would get to the South Seas. He would have to; there was no other place to land.

After finding a crew of four fellow Scandinavians to join him on his adventure, Dr. Heyerdahl traveled to South America. The first task was to find trees big enough to build an ocean-going raft. He had studied old pictures drawn by the Spanish conquistadors who had conquered Peru, and he knew that the Peruvian natives had built their rafts with a base of nine huge logs from balsa trees, which are exceptionally light. In those old days, the huge balsa trees had grown right near the coast, but now all of those forests had been cut down. Dr. Heyerdahl and his companions had to travel far into the jungles of Peru to find the large trees they needed. They cut down nine, stripped off all of the thick bark, and then floated their logs down a jungle river to the ocean. There, in a shipyard in Lima, the capital city of Peru, they built their raft.

First they laid the nine huge logs side by side and cut deep notches in each to make grooves to hold ropes. They lashed the logs together, and they tied ten more logs from smaller trees crosswise atop them. On top of that they made a deck by weaving together bamboo poles. Also from bamboo they constructed a little hut for some shelter from the fierce sun or rain. They erected two tall, slanted masts, and then on the rear of the raft, attached a huge single oar to use for steering. A large square sail was hung from the mast, and the vessel was christened *Kon Tiki*, after a legendary chieftain who was said to have led his people across the ocean to settle in the South Sea Islands.

The six men stocked their vessel with food for the journey, the same kinds of things that the ancient Incas would have taken: 200 coconuts, bags of sweet potatoes, gourds to hold water, and lots of different kinds of fruit. They also brought hooks, in the hope of catching fish along the way. In the small hut they installed a radio transmitter. They planned to send out messages of their progress. And they included an extra passenger: a fluffy green Amazon parrot named Lorita, who danced along the ropes that held the mast, eager for the voyage.

Now they were ready to begin their journey. Four thousand miles of open ocean lay before them. On April 28, 1947, the *Kon Tiki* set sail.

Because the *Kon Tiki* was a raft, it of course had no motor or engine to drive it forward. It had only the square sail. But Dr. Heyerdahl knew, as the ancient Incas must have known, that a steady wind blows always across the Pacific, from east to west, an unceasing current of air that would constantly fill the sail. As long as they wished to go west, the wind would take them that direction.

At first the men monitored the steering oar nervously and continuously, afraid that the vessel would go off course and wallow helplessly amongst the waves if they ceased to grip the oar. But soon they realized that the raft needed no such vigilance. The steady winds filled the sail, and the oar effortlessly steered the boat. All they needed to do was lash the oar to the deck so that it remained straight, and the *Kon Tiki* maintained her westward journey with little help needed from the men.

Despite this ease with steering, they were busy. The ropes that held the raft together must be constantly inspected, especially the lashes holding the big logs underneath the water. The repairing and replacing of rope became a large portion of each day's tasks, and the men dreaded the job of diving underneath the raft to fix the ropes there. The danger in this task was very real. The raft was moving at a steady speed, faster than a man could swim, and the raft could not be turned. A man left behind would never be able to catch up to the raft again. So any diver must attach himself with a long rope and take care to remain near the raft.

The other daily task was finding food. Some experts had warned Dr. Heyerdahl that fish would be scarce once the raft had left the shallower waters near land. After all, sailors on large ocean-going ships rarely saw large schools of fish. But soon the crew of the *Kon Tiki* realized that this expert opinion had been completely wrong. Fish teemed about the raft; to them it must have seemed a welcome shelter. Beneath the raft itself, scores of colorful fish spent their days keeping pace as the vessel floated westward; and every morning, the men would find their deck littered with flying fish who had been gliding forward during the night and landed helplessly aboard the raft. Flying fish became a favorite dinner for all the men aboard. All around *Kon Tiki,* sharks and dolphins and even large whales circled and cavorted, the sharks especially eager for any scraps of fish that the men might leave behind. In fact, the ever-present sharks presented an additional danger to whichever of the men was assigned the duty of inspecting the underwater ropes.

The raft glided westward. For the most part, the days passed smoothly. The men, after completing their work, read and talked, played guitar and sang. One of the crew spent his time crafting a careful model of the *Kon Tiki* out of little scraps of balsa wood. Every day, two men would work at sending out a radio message. One would turn a hand crank as fast as he could, to provide power, and the other would search for a signal. The *Kon Tiki* managed to make contact with amateur radio operators all over the world in places like California, New Zealand, and Norway, always politely asking them to pass their progress along to the Norwegian government, which was keeping track of their safety.

Once, when they had already gone more than two thousand miles, the raft was assaulted by a mighty ocean gale. For five days and nights the crew worked without sleep, hanging on to the steering oar with all their strength to keep the vessel pointed westward despite the raging, swirling wind. Their sail ripped, and their mast broke, but, when the storm passed, they repaired their damages and sailed on.

On the 92nd day of their journey, one of the crew men climbed to the top of the mast to scan the horizon, as was their daily custom. With a shout, he announced that he could see land! A low, green island lay to their right. They had reached the islands! Their voyage was a success!

Now the steady wind, which had been their strongest friend and ally, became their enemy, for try though they may, the men could not turn the raft. They wrestled all day with the oar and the sail, but the raft ignored their efforts and sailed serenely on to the west. The green island passed on their right and faded away behind them.

Four days later, another island appeared. Again they struggled, coming close enough to the island that some natives paddled out to them in canoes, climbed aboard, and tried to help them steer the raft to shore. But it was still no use. The wind drove them onward, the natives were forced to leave them and paddle back to their homes, and *Kon Tiki* continued her journey.

Finally, two days after that, they woke in the morning to discover a host of islands before them, and directly ahead they could see the surf breaking in huge sprays of foam against a large coral reef. The wind was driving them relentlessly forward, and they knew that they were going to crash onto the reef.

Frightened but resolute, they quickly stowed all of their most essential equipment in the little bamboo hut. They sent a last message, making contact with a radio operator in New Zealand. "We are going to be wrecked on a reef," they told him. "If you don't hear from us again in 36 hours, you will know that we have perished. Will you contact the Norwegian government if that happens?" The New Zealander promised that he would. The last words he heard from *Kon Tiki* were, "All right. Here we go."

You know, of course, that waves roll smoothly through the deep ocean water until they approach some land, which forces them upward until they curl over and crash in a pounding spray of surf. Twelve times, a cresting wave lifted the *Kon Tiki* and dashed it down atop the coral reef, and then sucked it back into the open water, only to hurl it forward again. The men aboard her clung to ropes, even as the hut collapsed and the steering oar and the masts snapped. Then a thirteenth wave seized the raft and flung it so far forward that it rested fully on the reef and remained there while the wave retreated. *Kon Tiki* had landed at last, and the men were safe.

Kon Tiki and her crew had traveled 3,770 miles in 101 days. They had shown without a doubt that the islands of the Pacific were indeed reachable for the people of ancient South America.

The raft was wrecked, but the nine huge balsa logs that formed her foundation were as sound as ever. *Kon Tiki* was repaired and towed to Tahiti, and from there, flown to Norway. If you ever should chance to visit that nation, you may go to the *Kon Tiki* Museum in Oslo and view the raft that proved Dr. Heyerdahl right.

Chapter 27

The Top of the World

Edmund Hillary and the rest of an English climbing team walked slowly into the capital city of Nepal, Kathmandu, in the heart of the great Himalayan Mountains. It had taken them nearly a month to get there, traveling first by airplane, then by train, then by rattling truck, and finally on foot. The city, that day in 1953, was an exotic place, different from any that Edmund had visited before, and for a young man from New Zealand, it was a different world. No roads led to it, only foot paths; and the streets teemed with merchants, goatherds, yaks, and Buddhist priests, but no cars or motorcycles. It would take many more weeks for the team's supplies to arrive, each load ferried separately on the backs of yaks. Edmund felt impatience scrabbling at his throat; as interesting as Kathmandu was, he was eager to continue on into the mountains, where every step would bring him closer to Everest, the tallest peak in the world, two hundred miles away. The team was planning to climb it, something that no man on earth had ever managed to do.

That long hike would require three weeks of walking steadily uphill, and it was important for the climbers to take their time, allowing their bodies to get used to the high altitudes. Even the foothills of the Himalaya mountains are higher than most places on earth, and unless they are born there, men's bodies do not work well in the thin air and low oxygen of the heights. A man's heart must work harder to pump his blood; his lungs must struggle to inhale and exhale. But by the end of their three-week walk up to Everest's knees, Edmund and the rest of the climbers were breathing easily; they were ready.

Climbing a mountain as huge as Everest is almost like fighting a war, with each separate part of the mountain providing its own battle to be won. First, the climbers needed to establish a base camp, a little city of tents from which they could launch their assault on the mountain. Like previous expeditions had done, they set their base right on top of the huge Khumbu Glacier, a mighty river of ice that flows down the valley on the southwestern side of Everest. Then they waited for the yaks bearing the rest of their supplies and contemplated the next battle to be fought: they must conquer the Khumbu Icefall.

Now, I am certain that most of my readers will have seen a waterfall, and so you know that it is a place where a river or stream drops suddenly from a high place to a lower one. Some waterfalls are small and delicate, and some thundering and awesome, but they are, most of them, dangerous: you wouldn't want to swim in one!

Knowing this about waterfalls, then, perhaps you can surmise the meaning of the term "icefall." If you are thinking that it is a place where ice is tumbling down from a higher elevation to a lower one, you are right! The Khumbu Glacier, in its slow journey down the valley, comes to a place where the valley narrows and becomes very steep. The ice, despite its slow speed, cracks and falls into huge blocks, some of them bigger than cars or houses. Giant cracks, called crevasses, open in the glacier, and sometimes climbers can hear the ice groaning as it moves over the icefall, and hear the gunshot-like cracks that it makes.

Does it sound like a frightening place? It is! And it was for Edmund and his fellows. Somehow they needed to find a way to climb up the icefall; the valley beyond was broad and smooth and would lead them directly to the upper face of Everest's peak. The danger was always near. Because the ice in a glacier is continually moving, ever so slowly, the blocks of ice in the icefall would often come crashing down with no warning, or suddenly shift and leave behind giant, yawning cracks. Edmund and the others began to climb through it, a little at a time, attaching ropes to spikes driven deep into the ice and bridging the cracks, which are called crevasses, with ladders and planks. After working at this all day, they would then have to climb back down to their base camp to rest overnight, and start again in the morning on the next section. Sometimes they would find that during the night a pinnacle of ice had fallen or a new crevasse had opened, and all their work from the day before would be lost.

As they labored together in the icefall, Edmund became better acquainted with a young Nepali man named Tenzing Norgay. Tenzing was a Sherpa, a native of the Himalayan region, and he had already climbed high on Everest's slopes several times. In fact, just one year before, Tenzing had accompanied a team of climbers from Switzerland in their attempt to conquer the mountain, and he and a Swiss climber had come within three hundred feet of the summit before high winds had forced them to turn back. Tenzing's experience had made him a valuable member of the English team.

One day, high up in the fall, Edmund and Tenzing came upon a small crevasse so small that Edmund shrugged and, taking a run at it, leaped across. But just as he landed on the other side, the lip of snow beneath him gave way, and he began to fall into the bottomless depths of the glacier. Thinking quickly, Tenzing, who was attached to Edmund with a rope, thrust his ice axe deep into the snow and wrapped the rope around it. The rope caught and held, abruptly stopping Edmund's headlong fall, and Tenzing was able to haul him up out of the crevasse and, thus, save his life.

As you can well imagine, Edmund was very grateful and also impressed with Tenzing's quick thinking and agility. He went to John Hunt, the leader of the expedition, and requested that he and Tenzing be considered as a partnership for the attempt on the summit.

Working slowly and methodically, the expedition made its way through the icefall and established another camp at its top. From there, they could look up the broad, high valley that would lead them to the mountain's ultimate peak. The valley is called the Western Cwm; that funny word, pronounced "coom," comes from the Welsh language and means "a bowl-shaped valley." It is also known as The Valley of Silence, because the massive face of Everest, high above, shelters the valley from the fierce winds that scour other parts of the Himalayas.

The Western Cwm's gently sloping floor was certainly easier for Edmund and his friends to climb, but it brought new challenges. The rounded, snow-covered sides of the valley caught and reflected the sun's bright rays, furiously burning the men's faces and blinding their eyes. At times, it was unbearably hot, over 90 degrees Fahrenheit. On such a warm day at your house, you might be thinking of going to a swimming pool to cool off, but there was no such option for the Everest climbers. As he helped the expedition move its camps ever higher, Edmund slung his down jacket around his waist and wore dark goggles to protect his eyes from the malevolent glare. And out of his pack he dug a present that his sister had given him: a striped sun hat crafted from a child's playsuit. For the rest of their time on Everest, the other members of the expedition could instantly identify Edmund by his jaunty striped hat!

The climbers spent two weeks at Camp 4, which was situated in the middle section of the Western Cwm, 21,200 feet above sea level. From there, they ranged ever higher, pitching tents and leaving supplies at camps all the way up to the top of the valley. There they set up Camp 8, at almost 26,000 feet high. Camp 8 was in the Death Zone.

That name sounds grim, doesn't it? Climbers use that term to describe any place above 25,000 feet, because a human being cannot survive more than a few days in such a place. The air is so thin, with so little oxygen, that the cells in the climber's body begin to die. Climbers in the Death Zone must be prepared to enter and leave it as quickly as possible.

Having established all of their camps, the expedition launched their final battle. On May 26th, four climbers, including John Hunt their leader, set out for the summit. Edmund and Tenzing and the rest of the team waited anxiously, huddled in the tents at Camp 8. They tried to sleep a little and conserve what strength they had, but it was difficult to do much of anything except worry and wonder how their companions were faring up on the peak. Finally, after many long hours, the four men stumbled back into the camp. They had carried a load of supplies up as far as they could, to a ledge at an elevation of 27,350 feet, and then two of them had gone on. But their tanks had run short of oxygen, leaving them no choice but to turn back. They had reached 28,700 feet, the highest that any human had ever climbed. But the summit had defeated them. Discouraged, John Hunt said to Edmund, "I don't believe that the summit ridge is climbable."

But Edmund, undaunted, prepared for his own attempt. On May 28th, he and Tenzing set out, climbing slowly, each breath painful in the thin air. They carried heavy packs, loaded with extra bottles of oxygen and a tiny tent, and when they reached 27,350 feet, they located the supplies that John Hunt had left a few days earlier. Adding those oxygen tanks to the ones they already carried, they forged upward. At 27,900 feet, they found a narrow sloping shelf, just wide enough for their tent. The wind howled about them as they struggled to erect it and then crawl inside. By Edmund's calculations, they had enough oxygen bottles to rest here for a few hours only, and then they must try to conquer the summit. They would get only one chance.

Early the next morning, the two men woke from a fitful sleep. The wind still roared. "Like a thousand tigers," Tenzing said. Edmund struggled to don his boots, only to find that they had frozen solid. An hour crawled by as they thawed the boots over the tiny flame of their miniature camp stove. Then in the dim early morning light, they set out.

Ever upward, step by step, they gained on the mountain's peak. Their steady progress was abruptly ended, however, when they came to a vertical cliff, 40 feet high. The summit was above it; somehow it must be surmounted, but how? Then Edmund noticed a crack, jagged and narrow, zigzagging up the cliff's face. It was barely wide enough to accommodate him, but he wriggled inside and climbed to the top, using every tiny handhold that he could find. Watching each move, Tenzing followed. It was surely the longest 40 feet of their entire climb. Ever after, this imposing cliff has been called the Hillary Step, in Edmund's honor.

Now the summit was in reach, up a ridge of snow. One after the other, they climbed the ridge until at last, at 11:30 A.M. on May 29, 1953, Edmund Hillary and Tenzing Norgay could climb no higher. They were standing at 29,035 feet. They had reached the top of the world.

They shared a heartfelt embrace, and Edmund pulled out his camera. He shot a picture of Tenzing staring out into the blue sky, and then took shots of the mountains in every direction, to provide proof that he and Tenzing had actually stood on the summit. Tenzing placed the flags of Nepal, India, and Great Britain in the snow, and after a last long look about them, they began their descent. They had been able to spend only fifteen minutes on the summit.

But in those fifteen minutes, Edmund and Tenzing became famous. As word reached the nations of the world that Everest had been climbed, a joyous celebration spread. The world's tallest mountain had been the world's last frontier, a place unseen by man. Now it, too, had been conquered. Men had reached every corner of the globe.

Chapter 28

Sputnik

S everal college students in New York City were working late one October evening in the university's radio station. Usually, they spent the night broadcasting music and news from their transmitter, but on this night in 1957 they were crowded around the station's receiver, listening intently to a strange "beep-beep-beep." One of the students was holding a tape recorder, trying to capture the sound as it grew louder, buzzing in their speakers, and then fading away. When the sound had disappeared entirely, the young men were deathly quiet for a moment, staring at each other with grim faces. Then they took the recorded tape they had made and set about rebroadcasting the beeping signal across America. When morning came, news of the signal was bellowed in huge newspaper headlines, and every American who heard that news felt afraid and uncertain. The world was a different place that next day, because of the signal that arched across the sky.

The "beep-beep-beep" was the voice of a little machine, a polished metal ball about two feet wide. It had two antennae attached, each with two parts, so that it looked rather like four long whiskers on either side of a round nose. Inside its shiny belly it carried a radio transmitter, with a battery to power it, and some sensitive thermometers to measure temperature. The whole sphere weighed 184 pounds, and when the college students and many others besides heard its signal, it was flying in orbit around the earth. It was named *Sputnik*, which means "satellite" in the Russian language; and that's just what it was: the first satellite made by man to fly in outer space.

If you were to look at a picture of *Sputnik*, I don't think you would find it very frightening. It looks almost like a child's toy. If you had been alive in 1957, you could have gone outside late at night and seen *Sputnik* gliding overhead, a tiny spark of light, not the least bit threatening. But to many people around the world, and especially to the people of the United States, it was a scary sight indeed. To them it meant that the Russians had gained a terrifying new power, and they feared that little *Sputnik* was a forerunner for rockets bearing huge, deadly bombs.

Are you wondering why they would be so afraid? To answer that question, I must take you back a few years, back into the 1940s, and I must tell you about the Cold War.

You will remember that, in order to defeat Adolf Hitler and end World War II, the United States and her Allies had worked together with Joseph Stalin, the dictator of Russia. Stalin had attacked Germany from the east and pushed forward all the way to the city of Berlin. So when the war ended, the Russians were in control of all of the nations of eastern Europe, including the eastern half of Germany. And Stalin intended to keep it that way. Despite his alliance with Winston Churchill of Britain and Franklin Roosevelt of the United States, he deeply distrusted them. He felt like his Russian army had been forced to do the greater amount of fighting against Hitler; after all, the Nazis had invaded Russia in 1941 and fought there for four terrible years. Russia had suffered cruelly. By the end of World War II, millions of Russians had died and many Russian cities had been destroyed. Stalin wanted to make sure that Russia was protected from invasion by taking over and occupying all the European nations along its western border.

At this point in history, Russia wasn't really even "Russia" any longer. Because of Vladimir Lenin and the Russian Revolution, Russia was a socialist nation, supposedly ruled by groups of workers called soviets, although in reality it was ruled by Stalin alone. Russia, along with all of the countries it had taken over, was called the USSR: the Union of Soviet Socialist Republics. This kind of government is also sometimes called communist, which comes from the word "common," because in a socialist country, no one owns anything. Everything is shared in common with everyone. There is not to be any rich or poor, nor any rulers or servants. Everyone is equal, and everyone does whatever the government leaders tell them to.

At least, that is the way most socialists would like it to be. In reality, though, it never really works out so neatly, because generally people do not like owning nothing and being equal, and they want to make up their own minds about what they would like to do. And so the communist nations of the world usually ended up with a very strong and oppressive government, in order to force the people to live in the communist way. Joseph Stalin's Russia was a brutal place, where secret police arrested and killed anyone who opposed the communist leader.

In the United States and Great Britain and other countries of the world who valued freedom for their citizens, the USSR was viewed with a great deal of alarm, especially when it began to press its socialist ways upon other nations. When all of eastern Europe was turned by the USSR into Socialist Republics, the United States recognized that they were facing a new and growing enemy.

But this new threat could not be directly attacked, because both the United States and the USSR had in their possession such terrible weapons that if they were to go to war with one another, they might very well destroy each other. So instead of fighting one another openly with fiery destruction, the two enemies battled each other in a "cold war": each sought to be better and stronger than the other in every way. They built up huge armies; they sent spies to steal secrets; they tried to convince other nations to be on their side. They even tried to best each other in sports and art, and most of all, in technology, which is the building of machines, especially weapons. And that is where little *Sputnik* comes back into this story.

When the Russians had entered the city of Berlin at the end of World War II, they had snatched up all of the Germans' knowledge and experience with rockets, which was quite a lot. They had taken this stolen information and given it to their own scientists, one of whom was a man named Sergei Korolev. He had been passionately interested in rockets since he had been a little boy, and now, for years, he had been working on rockets for Russia, making them more reliable and able to fly higher and capable of carrying heavier loads.

In May of 1954 Korolev went to the Minister of Defense, who was in charge of all of the USSR's weapons, and suggested that he begin working on a satellite to actually leave the earth's atmosphere and orbit around the globe in outer space. He didn't receive an answer right away, and so, went back to his usual work, hoping for the best. Just a few months later, the president of the United States, Dwight D. Eisenhower, announced that the Americans would be launching a satellite of their own. Immediately, Korolev was summoned and commanded to set to work at once on his satellite. The Minister of Defense wanted it to do more than just circle the globe: he wanted Korolev to make a satellite that would study the atmosphere around the earth, measure the rays coming from the sun, investigate the earth's magnetic field, and many other scientific projects. The satellite would have to be over ten feet long, and when all of the science instruments were put into its belly, it would weigh more than three thousand pounds! The parts for this big machine would be made in different workshops all over Russia, and then, Korolev was told, he must put it all together and blast it into space on the nose of a rocket. And he must do all of this before the Americans managed to put their own satellite into orbit.

Korolev did his best, but by the end of 1956, it was clear that the satellite could never be completed in time. The parts, coming from different places and made by different workmen, often did not fit together properly; and the rocket that was being prepared to launch the satellite into space was not going to be able to carry such a heavy load. Something different would have to be done.

Korolev feared that the Americans were going to beat them in this race into space. He suggested that they start over and build, instead, a very simple machine, whose only scientific instrument would be a thermometer. And so, over the course of one hectic month, little *Sputnik* came into being, a tiny silver ball that weighed less than two hundred pounds. The rocket would have no trouble lifting it into the sky.

On the night of October 4, 1957, *Sputnik* was launched. The rocket carried it effortlessly up through the atmosphere, and then, with a tiny explosion, separated from it so that it could fly forward on its own. The earth's gravity still held it, and so it flew in circles around the globe, completing its circle once every 96 minutes.

Down on the ground in the USSR, Korolev and his engineers waited anxiously. After just a few minutes they heard it: the "beep-beep-beep" of *Sputnik*'s radio transmitter, signaling that it was traveling safely along its path. They waited for 90 more minutes, to be sure that the satellite had made one complete trip around the earth, and then Korolev called the leaders of the USSR on the telephone to report their success. There was much celebration in Korolev's rocket lab that night!

But over in the United States, no one felt like celebrating. Because of the Cold War, the Americans feared that *Sputnik* was just a test, and that what the Russians were really doing was finding a way to launch a bomb from outer space to destroy them. In addition, the satellite's launch had come as a complete surprise, making everyone in America wonder what other grim surprises the USSR might have in store. Americans felt frightened and vulnerable, and also embarrassed. Since the end of World War II, the United States had become accustomed to thinking of itself as a "superpower," confident that its weapons were superior, that its security was assured, that it could not possibly be bested in any contest. But here was *Sputnik*, gliding overhead. Korolev had deliberately made his little satellite of the shiniest metal, so that it could be seen by anyone on the ground; and the USSR sent out a general message to all the radio operators of the world, telling them how they could listen to the satellite's signal. Millions of people listened, and millions more saw *Sputnik* winging its way along in its orbit. It was humiliating to the Americans that their nation did not have its own satellite to launch. And it was terrifying to them that their enemy could fly a strange machine through the sky right over their heads.

Sputnik continued to soar over the earth until January 4, 1958, when its speed began to lessen. It flew lower and lower, until finally it fell back into the earth's atmosphere and burned up. It had traveled around the earth 1,440 times.

But in the minds of both Russians and Americans, *Sputnik* lived on. In the United States, science and technology became more important than ever before. Young people were encouraged to study mathematics and science, and teachers were instructed to emphasize those subjects in their classrooms. The Americans were determined to win the next round of the Space Race; they were aiming to be the first to set foot on the moon, and they would not let the Russians beat them again. In the USSR, every Russian took pride in the satellite that had triumphed over the Americans. Russian scientists began working furiously on their project to launch a satellite with a human pilot inside.

So, as tiny as it was, *Sputnik* cast a very large shadow. Sputnik was the first step in a race that ended with an American named Neil Armstrong stepping out onto the surface of the moon.

Chapter 29

The Berlin Wall

If you were to visit Berlin, in Germany, you would see in various places throughout the city's center a strange row of cobblestones set into the surface of streets or running along the edges of sidewalks, sometimes turning a sharp corner right in the middle of a busy road. If you decided to follow them, you would find yourself taking a very long walk, for the cobbles trace a zigzag route that cuts the entire city in half, dividing it evenly into a western and eastern side. Once, you see, there was not just one Berlin, but two; and they were separated from each other by a towering wall. That wall is gone now. Although the cobblestones can show you where it once stood, they cannot tell you the wall's stories of sorrow and joy, and how it was built and torn down, each happening in the span of just one day.

At the end of World War II, the victorious Allied nations divided Germany into four parts, each one occupied by Great Britain, France, the United States, or the Russians. The same division was done in Germany's capital city, Berlin. The four nations agreed to rule over Germany until they felt they could allow the Germans to govern themselves once more.

There was little friendship between socialist Russia and the other three Allies. Russia, you remember, had become a communist country: the Union of Soviet Socialist Republics. Joseph Stalin wanted nothing more than to take over all of Germany and make it part of that Union. But the United States and Britain wanted Germany to eventually be free and independent, and they did not want communism to spread any further in the world. So though they had been an ally against Hitler, Stalin and the USSR were now an enemy. Stalin would never accept a free Germany.

So without Stalin's agreement, France, Great Britain, and the United States took the three parts of Germany that they had been occupying and combined them into a new country. It was called West Germany, and it was given its freedom and its own government. The USSR quickly responded by forming its portion of the old Germany into a new country as well, called East Germany. The city of Berlin was entirely within the new East German borders, but, remember, the city had been divided up amongst the four nations. So the Russians remained in control of East Berlin, but West Berlin became a little island of freedom in a socialist sea.

Despite the fact that it had been just one nation only a few years before and the same German people lived on both sides of the border, within a short time, West Germany became a very different place from East Germany. In the West, the land and the people recovered quickly from the terrible years of war with the help and support of the Allied nations. Shopkeepers expanded their shops, people repaired their homes or built new ones, farmers planted bountiful new crops and bought new machinery to harvest them. Housewives were able to use helpful new gadgets like washing machines; businessmen drove to work in the cities in gleaming new cars. Families could take vacations together, traveling all over Europe if they wished. West Germans, who called themselves *Wessies,* found that their lives were good.

But in East Germany, life was not good. The Russians had hated the Germans, who had invaded their nation in 1941 and caused such suffering. So instead of helping East Germany to heal from the war, the Russians took everything they could from it. Factory equipment, farm machines, even art and music, all were stripped away from East Germany and shipped back to the USSR. Even though East Germany was supposed to be its own country, it was really under the control of the Russians, and so its government became socialist. The East German people, the *Ossies,* had no freedom to make their lives better. They had to obey the communist leaders or face imprisonment or death; they could not travel, they could not start new businesses, they could not expand their shops or homes. East Germany was poor, and became poorer, and its people's lives were gray and sad.

People wanted out! And even though travel was forbidden, there was one way. West Berlin, like a little island in the middle of East Germany, offered the *Ossies* a path of escape to West Germany and freedom. Hundreds of thousands of East Germans packed their bags and headed for West Berlin. Even though some of them were stopped along the way, most of them were able to make it across the border into the western half of the city. Once there, the West Berliners put them in airplanes and flew them to safety in West Germany.

By 1961 East Germany had lost two and a half million of its citizens. If something wasn't done, there would not be anyone left in the country! The communist leaders of East Germany could see the obvious place to stop this huge exodus. So with the USSR behind them, the East German government attempted to take control of West Berlin. But the United States and other free countries realized what the communists were trying to do, and they sent a strong message: do not even try it. We will defend West Berlin with open warfare if necessary.

East Germany and the USSR did not want to risk that. So the leaders of East Germany decided to try something else.

Shortly past midnight on August 13, 1961, huge trucks filled with soldiers and construction workers rumbled through the streets of East Berlin. They began to tear up the roadways that entered into West Berlin. They dug deep holes and put up giant concrete posts, and then strung razor-sharp barbed wire all across the border between East and West Berlin. Then they cut the telephone wires that led between the two halves of the city. When Berliners on either side of this new barrier awoke, they were shocked to discover that their city was cleft in two.

The people of Berlin had been used to easily traveling back and forth; *Ossies* went into West Berlin every day for concerts at the opera house or shopping in the well-filled stores. Families and friends lived on either side of the border and visited each other frequently. But no more. If a Berliner had gone to sleep that night on the eastern side of the border, then on the eastern side he would stay, for the next 28 years.

The new wall ran for more than one hundred miles, straight through the center of the city and then wrapping in a circle entirely around West Berlin, so that it was cut off completely from the rest of East Germany. Though it started out as concrete posts and barbed wire, within just a few days the East German government had replaced it with an even sturdier structure: a tall wall built of concrete blocks, topped with coils of barbed wire. Then, in 1965, this barrier in turn was taken down and an even taller concrete wall was built, supported by huge bars of steel. By 1975 the Berlin Wall was changed yet again and made all the more threatening. Now it was built of concrete slabs, twelve feet high and four feet wide. A smaller inner wall was built three hundred feet away, and the space between was a terrible trap, with trenches and lights, watchtowers and electric wires, soldiers patrolling with dogs and watchful guards armed with guns, who had orders to shoot anyone trying to get past the wall into West Berlin.

There were nine gates in the wall, where soldiers or government leaders could travel back and forth, but which no East Berliner was allowed to pass. The towering wall did indeed do the job it was built for; it prevented most *Ossies* from escaping East Germany. But it did not prevent all of them. During the 28 years that the wall cast its shadow over Berlin, almost five thousand people made it safely across.

At first, the escape attempts were simple. Some simply threw a rope over the wall and climbed up and over. Others drove a truck or bus straight into the wall and then ran for West Berlin with all their might. Others risked gravely injuring themselves by jumping out of the windows of tall apartment buildings that bordered the wall.

But as the wall became taller and stronger, the East Berliners who wanted to escape were forced to come up with more complicated plans. Some people dug tunnels under the wall from the basements of buildings in East Berlin. Another group of people gathered all the scraps of cloth they could find and stitched them together to make a hot-air balloon with which they glided over the wall to land safely on the other side. Some tried using hang gliders from tall nearby roofs or creeping through the sewer system that ran beneath the streets.

Not all were successful. Some died while trying to escape, either because their plan was too risky or because they were killed by the soldiers guarding the wall.

But after 28 years, the wall fell just as suddenly as it had risen. In 1988 and 1989, the people in many communist countries began to throw off their socialist governments and demand lives of more freedom. Communism began to falter and then to fade in all of Russia's border countries: Poland, Hungary, Czechoslovakia. East Germany found itself standing rather alone, with neighbors who were no longer communist and who were eager to welcome any East German who wanted to leave. The country could no longer force all of its unhappy people to stay.

Suddenly, on the evening of November 9, 1989, the East German government made a simple announcement: Any East Berliner who wanted to could cross over into West Berlin.

At first the people were in shock. Could this really be true? Were the gates in the wall truly open? Cautiously, East Berliners began to approach the fearsome wall and found that indeed the guards were allowing people to cross. First a few and then dozens and then hundreds of *Ossies* ran through into West Berlin, where they found hundreds of *Wessies* waiting for them. A joyous celebration began, with family and friends who had not seen each other for 28 years weeping and hugging, cheering and singing. Young people began to dance along the top of the wall, and others brought hammers and chisels and began chipping pieces off.

Eventually, the citizens of both East and West Berlin removed the wall, both by pulling down huge slabs or by breaking off little fragments. Today, in Berlin, the only memory of the wall can be found in the cobblestones inlaid in the streets that trace its route and in a small portion left standing as a memorial to those who died trying to cross it.

As for East Germany, it also has disappeared. East and West Germany were brought back together into a single German nation on October 3, 1990, and that is how Germany remains to this day. The Germans are once again one people, as they always wished to be, and the dark memory of the Berlin Wall has begun to fade away.

Chapter 30

New Lands

T he next time that you are playing outside, running barefoot on a warm day, I want you to stop for a moment and wiggle your toes in the grass. Think about the layers of dirt and rock that stretch below your feet. They seem unchangeable, don't they? The hills and valleys that surround your town, the river that rolls under the bridge and away toward the sea, and the dirt and rock beneath them all; all of it appears established and changeless.

But actually, as I am sure you know, our earth is a restless place. Wind and water can erode even the largest boulder, rivers can change their course, and earthquakes can shake solid stone. The rocks and dirt are constantly reshaped, mostly very slowly, but sometimes with alarming suddenness. This makes the study of our planet a very exciting pursuit, a science called geology. And perhaps no geologist has had quite so much to examine in the last 70 years as the vulcanologist: the scientist who investigates volcanoes. That is because the twentieth century has been full of volcanic happenings. Let me tell you about two of them.

On the morning of February 20, 1943, a farmer named Dionisio Pulido rose early with his wife Paula. On their little plot of land in the center of Mexico, the Pulido family grew corn and peppers, and today they were planning to burn some shrubbery that was creeping into their cornfield. Along with their young son, they had just begun to pile up the offending branches, when suddenly, all three of them heard a loud bang. Looking up in surprise, they saw the earth in front of them open up in a gaping crack. Dreadful hissing noises arose out of the crevice, and the air around them suddenly stank with the smell of rotten eggs.

The smell was actually sulfur gas, a chemical that forms deep within the earth. The crack that opened in front of the family's eyes would soon become something much greater.

If the ground split open right in front of you, what do you think you would do? The Pulido family scattered in fear. Later, Dionisio described how he felt: "I was so stunned I hardly knew what to do or what to think. I couldn't find my wife or my son or my animals. I ran to see if I could save my family, but I could not see them. I was very frightened, and I mounted my mare and galloped to the village where I found my wife and son and friends waiting for me. They were afraid that I was dead and that they would never see me again."

All that night, the villagers huddled together, listening to huge booms and thuds and explosions. Many of them thought that the world was surely ending. The next day Dionisio and the other villagers cautiously crept back to the farm to see what was happening. To their amazement, a cone-shaped hill taller than several houses had swallowed Dionisio's cornfield. With explosive bangs, the cone was throwing up rocks and glowing cinders, and it seemed to be growing larger even as they watched.

The villagers ran back to their little town. They began to pack their few belongings, worried. Would the cone continue to expand?

It did. By the end of that week, it was three hundred feet tall. Fine gray ash blanketed the whole village, and some horses and cows died from breathing it. The people knew that they would have to leave. By June the last villagers had walked sadly away, looking back at their homes, with the ominous cone looming behind, sending up a huge plume of glowing smoke. Just in time they left, for a short while later the volcano began to ooze lava, red-hot melted rock. A river of lava flowed over the village, covering it completely, engulfing a nearby town as well. All that remained were two church towers standing forlornly above a sea of black, hardened lava.

For the next nine years, the volcano continued to erupt, building itself ever higher. It was given the name Paricutin, after the village where the Pulido family and their friends had lived. Finally, when it had reached a height of 1,400 feet, it grew quiet. Vulcanologists who have studied it believe that it is dead now, never to erupt again. It stands today in the middle of Mexico, a brand-new mountain where a small village and a little farm growing corn and peppers used to be.

A few years later and many miles away, a small fishing boat bobbed in the waves off the coast of Iceland. It was an early November morning in 1963, and the crew had been working since long before dawn, hoping to snare a large catch of cod. Their cook, a man named Olafur, came out onto the deck, squinting his eyes at the horizon. Far in the distance he thought he saw something: a wisp of smoke or steam. He hurried to fetch the captain, who gazed at the gray smudge for a moment and then declared that they must alert the Iceland Coast Guard at once, because it must be another ship on fire.

The Coast Guard radio operator was puzzled, though, when he received the call. He had gotten no requests for help that morning. Surely a boat on fire would have sent out a distress call. Nevertheless, the operator dispatched a crew of Coast Guardsmen to see for themselves if someone was in trouble.

As the Coast Guard boat drew near the column of smoke, the men on board realized that this was not a burning ship. They could hear the booming echo of explosions and see the arching trails of burning rocks hurled up into the sky. This was a volcano, coming straight up out of the ocean!

Three hours later a huge cloud of smoke and ash towered 12,000 feet up into the sky, growing taller every minute. By that afternoon, the eruption could be seen in Iceland's capital city, Reykjavik, which was miles away. The next day the Coast Guardsmen went out again to study the boiling smoke. This time, using their binoculars, they could see a low hump of dark, steaming rock rising above the waves: a new island!

For the next few months, the volcano continued to throw out huge amounts of glowing pebbles and ash, a mixture of material that vulcanologists call "tephra." On April 4th lava began to stream out of the crater, sometimes shooting upward in fountains two hundred feet high. It ran down into the sea where the water hissed and let out enormous clouds of steam. The lava also flowed toward the ocean in long tunnels, so that even today the island is riddled with caves like a giant round sponge. The lava continued to spew out and the tephra to pile up for four more years until the eruption finally stopped on June 5, 1967. By now the island had a name: Surtsey, after a fire giant named Surt in old Icelandic legends.

Geologists all over the world were thrilled to have the chance to study the birth and life of a brand new volcano. The government of Iceland made it illegal for anyone to set foot on Surtsey except for scientists, so the island is like a giant science experiment, where they can observe and measure everything that happens there.

At first, the geologists were worried that the island would not survive. It was only a large pile of lava and tephra, after all, and the occan's waves might pound it to pieces in just a few months. But as the lava continued to flow, and the island grew bigger and more sturdy, the scientists began to hope that it would become permanent. By the end of the eruption, Surtsey stretched over almost two square miles.

As geologists began to wander over the new island, they were amazed by what they found. Landscapes that they had thought took thousands of years to form had appeared almost at once: wide sandy beaches; tall craggy cliffs; gravel banks; still, silent lagoons; boulders already worn smooth by the relentless ocean. Surtsey was only a few years old and she looked as if she had always been there.

Geologists were not the only ones eager to examine Surtsey. The island was also a thrilling opportunity for biologists, who are scientists that study living things. Because Surtsey had started out as completely barren, steaming rock, biologists could watch carefully and see what kinds of life appeared on the new land.

Even before the eruption had stopped, seagulls had been landing on the rock, resting before continuing on to Iceland. By the summer of 1964, biologists were already seeing flies and moths. After 1967 moss began to grow on the rocks, giving the gray island a robe of color for the first time. The first bird's nest was spotted by a biologist in 1970, and now twelve species of birds regularly nest there. Many kinds of birds have learned to use Surtsey as a temporary stop on their migration journeys. Seeds carried by birds and by ocean currents also took root, and today there are 69 different kinds of plants growing on the island.

If you would like to visit Surtsey, you will need to become a geologist or a biologist, since they alone are allowed ashore. The ocean waves have eroded the island somewhat, but it is still robed in colorful moss, home to birds and butterflies. Fifty years ago it was a column of smoke rising from the sea, but today it is a place of study and solitude, its only building a tiny cabin where scientists camp while doing their work.

So this is a marvelous thing to know about our planet: a farmer's cornfield or a stretch of cold ocean water can become brand-new land. Even if such a change is frightening, as I am sure Dionisio Pulido and his family would say, it can also bring new life. When a baby bird pokes its head out of a nest on Surtsey's cliffs, the biologist who is watching nods in satisfaction. Change might be alarming or it might be exciting, but it is always part of our life here on earth.

Chapter 31

Old Thrones

I suspect that if I were to ask you to think about a king, you would picture in your mind a monarch from days of yore, dressed in heavy royal robes with an enormous crown upon his head. You might think of him surrounded by knights in armor or a room full of glittering courtiers wearing hats with long plumes. But did you know that in our modern world, there are 44 countries that are still ruled by kings or queens? Though nowadays they often dress in suits and ties and their attendants no longer wear plumes, they still sit upon the thrones of their fathers, and some of them come from lines of kings that stretch back over a thousand years.

For most of mankind's history, and well into the years of the nineteenth century, most nations on earth were ruled by kings. But after 1775, when George Washington declined to be named King of the United States, the people of many countries put an end to kingship, sometimes peacefully and sometimes with great violence. Nations that kept their kings often decided to limit the king's power, so that even though he is the monarch, he is yet subject to the laws and rules of his nation. That is the case in the 44 nations that continue to have a king or queen up to this day.

The oldest monarchy in the world is the Imperial House of Japan. The Emperor of Japan is the latest member of a family that has been ruling over the island nation since 660 years before the birth of Christ. That is a very old family indeed! They are a dynasty, which means a ruling family. For 2,700 years each emperor in Japan has passed his crown down to his son, without any breaks in the line. Isn't that an amazing feat?

The first emperor was named Jimmu. He has become a legend in Japan, where they say that he was a grandson of the sun goddess Amaterasu. He battled several other local leaders to become king of Japan, and the place where he won his last victory was called Yamato; thus, the family was known from that day forward as the Yamato Dynasty. Jimmu was crowned king on February 11, 660 B.C., and the Japanese people still celebrate that date as the Foundation Day of their nation. From the time of Jimmu, 125 emperors have ruled over Japan. Their seat of kingship is called the Chrysanthemum Throne. In the Japanese language, the Emperor is called *Tenno*, which means the Heavenly Sovereign. His name is never used by any Japanese person; instead he is always called His Majesty the Emperor.

For much of Japan's history, the emperor was not a warrior or a lawgiver. The job of leading armies in battle, running the government, and making laws fell to a different man, called the shogun, who was given his power by the emperor's decree. The emperor concerned himself mostly with writing poetry and painting calligraphy. But when ships from England and the United States came to Japan in the 1800s, demanding that the island nation open its ports for trade or face the threat of war, the shoguns of that time were unable to stop them or drive them away. The Japanese people, just like their Chinese neighbors, did not want to allow any strangers into their nation, and their anger at the shoguns' failure spurred them to demand that the Emperor himself do the work of leading them. In 1868 Japan got rid of the shoguns; now the Emperor himself would lead their armies and make their laws. The king at that time was the Emperor Meiji, so this change in the Japanese government is called the Meiji Restoration, because all the power in Japan was restored to the Emperor.

In 1926 the Chrysanthemum Throne passed to Meiji's grandson, whose name was Hirohito. In his early years as Emperor, Hirohito ruled over a nation that was growing ever more warlike. The Army and Navy had great power, and Japan was eager to stretch its boundaries, as you learned when you read about World War II. With Hirohito's agreement, the Japanese Army invaded China in 1937 and then entered into alliance with Nazi Germany and Italy to form the Axis Powers. But still, when his advisors began to urge him to enter into war with the United States and Great Britain, Hirohito hesitated. At a meeting with the leaders of his army, he quoted for them a poem written by his grandfather, the Emperor Meiji:

Across the four seas, all are brothers.

In such a world why do the waves rage, the winds roar?

Gradually though, Hirohito changed his mind. Japan needed more resources, and to get them she felt that she must expand her empire and invade her neighbors. The United States stood in the way of such a plan, so the United States must be removed from Japan's path. When his advisors came to him with a scheme to attack the American Navy at Pearl Harbor, in Hawaii, he approved the idea and committed his nation fully to war.

For the first six months, the Japanese won every battle against the Americans. But as the tide of the war began to change, in 1942 and 1943, Hirohito could see that Japan was in danger. He urged his army and navy to fight harder, and he hid the truth from his people. Until the end of the war, the losses that the Japanese suffered were reported as great victories. Only when American bombers began attacking their cities did the people realize that their situation was very grim. On July 26, 1945, the Allies sent a message to the Emperor telling him that Japan must surrender at once. Hirohito refused, and it seemed to the Americans that the Japanese would never stop fighting, and many lives would be lost if the war continued. So to end the war, the United States dropped two bombs on the Japanese cities of Nagasaki and Hiroshima.

They were atomic bombs, a new kind of weapon which caused an enormous explosion by splitting apart an atom. Each tiny atom in the universe is held together by vast amounts of energy, and when the particles that make up an atom are forced apart, that energy is unleashed in a towering ball of fire. The two bombs completely destroyed the Japanese cities.

On August 15, 1945, the Japanese people gathered around their radios heard the Emperor Hirohito tell them that he had decided to surrender. It was the first time the Emperor's voice had ever been heard by the common people of Japan. He told them that they must "endure the unendurable" and accept the surrender.

After the war, many outside of Japan demanded that Hirohito be put on trial for the terrible things that had happened during the war. Some in his own family said that he should stand aside and allow the crown prince Akihito to become Emperor. Hirohito remained on the throne, but he was no longer the powerful king he had been. The Japanese changed their government after the war, removing all true power from the Emperor and making him a figurehead. This means that the Emperor is a symbol for the Japanese, of their nation and of their unity as a people. He is also the head of the Japanese Shinto religion. Japan is ruled now by a Prime Minister and a parliament, who are elected by the voting of the people.

But the people of Japan still revere their Emperor. Since 1989, when Hirohito died, his son Akihito has sat upon the Chrysanthemum Throne. He has made an effort to bring the Imperial family closer to the common Japanese people. He and his wife have visited every corner of Japan. When Japan suffered a terrible earthquake and tsunami in 2011, Akihito appeared on television in a recorded message, something that had never been done before, and urged the people not to give up hope and to help each other. He and his wife also visited a shelter where people were gathered after the disaster, hoping to inspire them. Just a few months later, despite the sadness which the earthquake had caused, the Japanese lined the streets to cheer for the Emperor's 73rd birthday. When Akihito is gone, his son will become the Heavenly Sovereign in his place, and the line of Japanese kings will continue onward just as it has done for almost three thousand years.

In 1953, just after he had been formally named the crown prince, Akihito left Japan in a journey halfway around the world to attend the coronation of another monarch, Queen Elizabeth II of United Kingdom. She also sits upon a very old throne.

Four countries make up the United Kingdom: England, Scotland, and Wales—which together are called Great Britain—and Northern Ireland. In the earliest years of the Middle Ages, before the year 1000, most of the isle of Britain was ruled by Anglo-Saxon kings. When William the Conqueror overpowered England in 1066, he began a new line of kings that has continued up to this day. For a while, the four countries continued to have separate rulers, but gradually they were all brought under one crown. In 1200 the nation of Wales was absorbed into England. In 1603 the Scottish king James I became king of England as well, and in 1707 Scotland and England were united into the nation of Great Britain. Ireland joined them in 1801 to form the United Kingdom. By then, Great Britain was also master of colonies and territories all over the world. The British king was ruler of a vast empire, which by 1921 covered one-fourth of the world's surface.

During the 1920s most of the United Kingdom's colonies, while still loyal to the British king, wished to become independent nations of their own and were given the right to do so. Gradually, the British empire diminished until just 14 overseas territories were left, places like Canada, Australia, New Zealand, and several islands in the Caribbean Sea. These joined together in a group of nations that called themselves the Commonwealth; they were independent countries who governed themselves, but nonetheless they still considered the British king to be their head and the symbol of their friendship and equality with each other.

In Ireland, meanwhile, the Irish leaders decided that they no longer wished to be a part of the United Kingdom. In 1928 the whole southern portion of Ireland seceded: this means that it officially broke away from the kingdom and became its own country, the Republic of Ireland. But the northern portion of the island remained a part of the kingdom, a situation which made some of its people happy and some very angry indeed. For the next 50 years, Northern Ireland would be rocked by fierce battles between those who wished to remain British and those who yearned for independence. Eventually, Northern Ireland was given its own government and leaders, but it continued to be a part of the United Kingdom. The battles subsided, and Northern Ireland is at peace today.

In 1936 a new king ascended to the British throne, Edward VIII. He was young and strong, and his people expected him to rule for many years and lead them through the storm of war that they could see was coming. But Edward wished to marry an American lady of whom the leaders of the kingdom could not approve. So Edward did something most unexpected: he gave up his throne. He married his American wife and left Great Britain. The throne was left to his brother, who certainly never expected to have it. He was crowned King George VI. As the dark shadows of World War II enveloped his country, George became an inspiration. From childhood he had suffered from a terrible stammer; he could hardly speak three words together without halting and stuttering. But he overcame this handicap to speak to his people on the radio constantly throughout the war. He visited the soldiers as they prepared to go into battle, and the areas of London that were bombed by the Nazis.

George and his wife Elizabeth had two daughters: Elizabeth and Margaret. Following her father's example, the Princess Elizabeth did all she could to encourage the British people during those dark days. In 1940 she sent out a radio message especially for the children of Britain: "Try not to be afraid," she said. "In the end, all will be well." In 1945, when she was 19 years old,

Elizabeth joined the war effort and learned to be an ambulance driver and a mechanic. She is the only head of state in the world today who served in uniform during World War II.

Despite his tireless efforts during the war, George was not a healthy man, and Elizabeth knew that she must be prepared to become queen even as a very young lady. On her 21st birthday, she sent out a message to all the nations of the Commonwealth: "I declare before you all that my whole life, whether it be long or short, shall be devoted to your service and the service of our great imperial family to which we all belong."

George VI died in 1952, and his daughter became Elizabeth II. For 60 years she has reigned as Queen of the United Kingdom. She has witnessed many of the events that you have read about in these stories. She saw Hitler defeated and the nation of Israel created; on the morning of her coronation, word reached London that Edmund Hillary and Tenzing Norgay had conquered Mount Everest. She witnessed the flight of *Sputnik* and the fall of the Berlin Wall. Through all the world's changes over the course of all those years, she has remained steady and unswerving, quietly devoted to doing her duty. She and her husband, Prince Philip, have visited every nation of the Commonwealth many times, making her the most widely traveled monarch in history. She meets with England's Prime Minister every week to discuss the needs of the nation. She is the head of Great Britain's Armed Forces; all British soldiers look forward to the day once a year when the Queen inspects the troops. She is the governor of the Church of England, and one of her titles is Defender of the Faith.

The year 2012 marks Elizabeth's Diamond Jubilee: her 60 years on the ancient throne of Great Britain. Millions of people will line the streets of London to celebrate their much-loved Queen.

So kingdoms endure, even in our modern world. Both Akihito and Queen Elizabeth walk a path that stretches back into the pages of history and forward into the years to come.

Chapter 32

The Channel Tunnel

W hen England's greatest writer, William Shakespeare, thought of his home, he wrote about it this way: "This scepter'd isle, this earth of majesty . . . This fortress built by Nature for herself, against infection and the hand of war, this little world, this precious stone set in a silver sea, which serves it in the office of a wall, or as a moat defensive to a house." Can you picture what he is saying? Unlike the rest of Europe, England has always been an island, protected from enemies and danger by the sea that surrounds it. Its closest neighbor is France, which it faces across a narrow, thirty-mile stretch of ocean called the English Channel.

For more than two hundred years, both Englishmen and Frenchmen have proposed the idea of a tunnel underneath the waters of the Channel to connect little England to France, and thus to the rest of Europe. The French emperor Napoleon was the first to suggest it, in the year 1802, and a French engineer quickly seized upon the idea, drawing up plans for a tunnel braced with wood and lit by candles, through which coachmen could drive their horses and provide travelers with a quick, but dark and smoky, journey underneath the sea. Relations between France and England were none too friendly, though, and the technology to dig such a fearsomely long and deep tunnel did not really exist at that time. The idea quickly became a joke, and then was abandoned.

As time went by and railroads began to crisscross Europe,

churning steam locomotives were soon a familiar sight. Travelers could now easily make their way from London to Paris and beyond, but the Channel was always in their way. The only way to cross its choppy waters was aboard tiny ferry boats, a method of transportation that left most travelers queasy and exhausted. The Channel crossing was the most hated portion of the trip.

But engineers were gaining experience in constructing long tunnels. Mines were delving ever deeper into the earth all across England. In 1843 a tunnel underneath the Thames River in London was engineered, proving that tunnels could indeed be constructed underneath bodies of water; and then, in 1869 the Suez Canal opened, showing, as you have read, that huge engineering projects could be successfully completed, as long as the builders were given enough money and time.

So once again engineers in both France and England began rethinking the Channel tunnel idea. They were more confident now, in both their knowledge and in the machines and technology available to them. Putting their heads together, they began to work through the problems facing a tunnel of this magnificent size.

First, they must consider the rock underneath the Channel's waters. Was it stable and firm or cracked and brittle? In order to burrow the 30 miles from England to France, they would need a solid layer of a single kind of rock. On both the English and French sides of the Channel, tall white cliffs of chalk rose up like beacons, exactly the same sort of chalk with which you write upon a blackboard. They would need to be certain that the solid chalk ran under the seabed as well. The chalk would be perfect for tunneling because it was waterproof and strong.

Second, they must figure out how to fill the tunnel with fresh air. Remember, in the 1800s the trains were powered by steam and coal, and belched black plumes of smoke from their stacks as they hurtled down the track. Without some sort of ventilation system, the tunnel would quickly fill with smoke and choke the train's passengers and crew. But how do you fill a tunnel with fresh air when that tunnel is below the floor of the sea?

Third, the leaders of the English government were worried about the risk to their island that the tunnel would pose. Just like Shakespeare three hundred years before, they saw England as a castle with the ocean surrounding her as a moat, protecting her from any enemy. What if the tunnel fell into the hands of a hostile foe? The Englishmen did not want to worry about an army of invaders creeping out of the tunnel to surprise them in the darkness of some summer night!

By the 1870s both England and France had set up tunnel companies to work on these problems, and on both sides of the channel, the companies were surveying the rock beneath the water. First they dug shafts, long narrow holes, into the rock on the shore to check if the chalk layer ran deep enough. On the English side, the holes stayed clear and dry, but on the French side, they filled with seawater at once; there were cracks in the chalk layer somewhere under the Channel. The French engineers switched to a different location and tried again. This time the shafts stayed dry; now they knew where to begin digging from both sides. In 1881 the digging began, using giant boring machines, which look rather like enormous screws.

By 1882 they had dug more than one mile into the chalky seafloor on either side. But in England, the fear of invasion grew ever stronger. To many people, especially the generals who led England's armies, the tunnel seemed like an open invitation to her enemies. In 1883 a law was passed that forbade the English Tunnel Company to do any further digging. In vain the company tried to protest. They offered to dig a porthole halfway through, and station a soldier there 24 hours a day. If anyone tried to invade, the soldier would open the port and flood the tunnel! But this offer did no good; the leaders of England wanted nothing more to do with the Channel Tunnel. The French gave up, as well. They assumed the English would always be too stubborn to risk the well-being of their "island fortress."

Then came the Great War. Oh, how England's generals wished now that they had a tunnel! Throughout the dreadful years of the war, England's soldiers and supplies, her food and guns and equipment, all had to cross the open waters of the Channel under constant gunfire from enemy ships. How many lives were lost that a tunnel would have saved! Some of England's leaders said later that the Great War might have been as much as two years shorter if the tunnel had been built in 1882.

After the World Wars, as the twentieth century moved forward, talk of building the tunnel continued, off and on. But it was not until the 1980s that the English and the French once again began to consider it seriously. The two governments sent scientists to study the sea floor. By this time in history, technology was all the more advanced; now engineers could use computers and sonar machines to look deep under the earth, and they determined that the chalk layer did indeed run all the way across from England to France. Huge boring machines were assembled on both sides, which the English referred to with numbers, but which the French gave lovely names: Brigitte, Europa, Catherine, Virginie, Pascalin'e, and Séverine.

The digging took six years. The engineers constructed not one tunnel, but three: two large tunnels for the trains, one going each way, and between them a smaller tunnel, which would be an escape route if there were to be a fire or other disaster in one of the main tunnels. The small tunnel was bored first to be certain that the chalk was firm and stable enough, then the big tunnels on either side.

In 1994 with the tunnel completed, two trains swept toward it from either side. One carried Elizabeth, the Queen of England, and the other Francois Mitterand, the president of France. Elizabeth's train whisked through the tunnel to emerge on the French side, where the trains met, nose to nose. With great dignity, the two leaders emerged and met in the center of the track where they cut a large ribbon to announce to the world that the Channel Tunnel was officially open.

Except that it wasn't, really. It took several more months of work before the Chunnel, as the newspapers began calling it, was ready for regular use.

Now that it is in business, though, the Chunnel is very popular. A passenger on the high-speed train that races through the tunnel can make the journey from London to Paris in only 2 hours and 15 minutes. The train travels at 186 miles per hour! Since the tunnel opened in 1994, trains have carried 8 million travelers, 4 million cars, 1 million trucks, and 4 million tons of goods from England to France and back again.

The tunnel has had its share of troubles, though. One winter night in 2009, the coldest night in eight years, five trains heading across France toward London encountered a heavy fall of fluffy snow. The snow built up on the tops and sides of the trains, and when they left the cold behind and entered the warmer air of the Channel Tunnel, the snow began to melt. The water caused the electric wires on the trains to fail, and they all broke down inside the tunnel. Two thousand passengers had to spend the night down in the Chunnel's belly, without any food or water, until rescuers could haul the malfunctioning trains out of the tunnel with a large gas-powered engine. One of the liberated travelers described the night she had just spent as a "complete nightmare!"

But despite such mishaps, thousands of people travel through the Channel Tunnel every day. Perhaps only a few of them pause each day to marvel at the tunnel that whisks them between England and France. It is one of the largest construction projects ever undertaken by man. So much chalk was removed by the boring machines that it actually increased the size of Great Britain: a park was made with the debris that is as large as 68 football fields. Thirteen thousand workers labored in its construction.

As you may have noticed, in our tales of the nations, when men are resolved to accomplish a goal, they often succeed. Perhaps, more than war and conflict, perseverance and determination are the true stories of the modern world.

We have made a long journey together, haven't we, through the nineteenth and twentieth centuries? Those years have ushered in a world that has been transformed by science and discovery, exploration and war. If you were to ask your grandmother and grandfather to tell you their tales of the world when they were young, I suspect that both you and they would be amazed at the changes that have taken place just during their lifetimes.

I wonder how many of you can think back to the very first story in this book, where you learned that the world we live in is called "modern" because of all the history that came before. In many ways, history is like a sleek train flashing through the Channel Tunnel: It begins its journey in one place, dives beneath the surface of the sea, and then emerges somewhere very different. The stories of history begin in the past—sometimes very far away in the past; sometimes just yesterday—and then dive beneath the present day and emerge to go racing off into the future. From where you sit, reading this book today, you might not think that you are a part of history; but you are. Someday when you are grown you may look back in amazement at all the history that has been stretching out behind you since you were a child. Just like a train, history is always moving forward, collecting its many wondrous stories to share with some other child who is waiting, farther down the track.

Helpful Maps

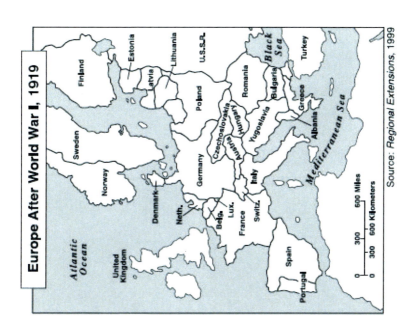

Europe After World War I, 1919

Source: *Regional Extensions*, 1999

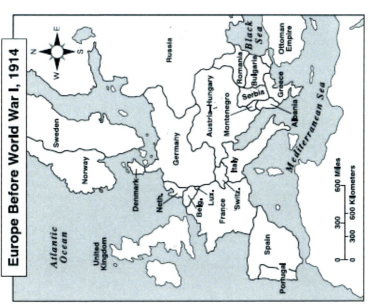

Europe Before World War I, 1914

Europe in 1940

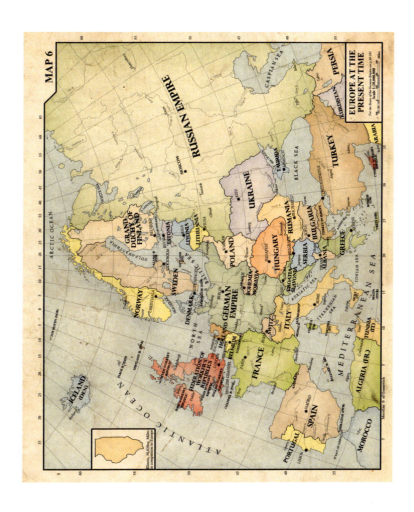

Modern Europe

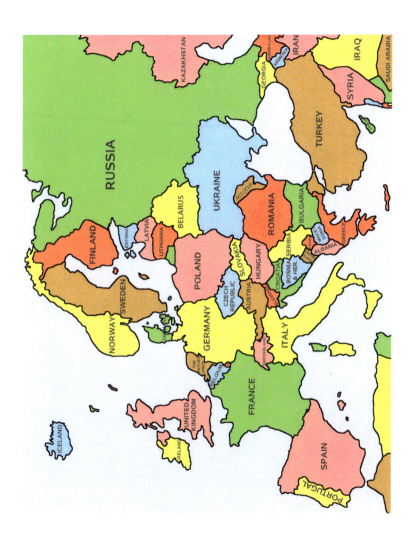

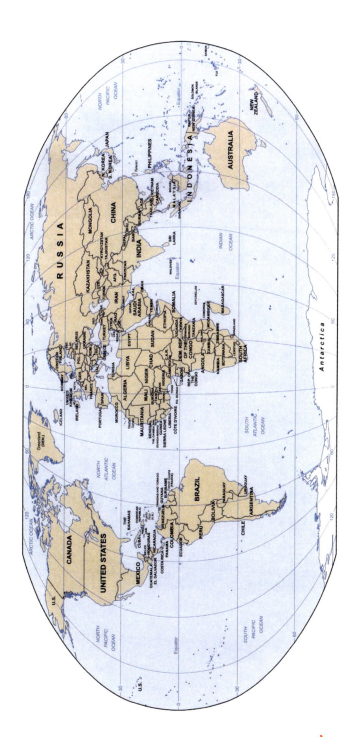